MARIE CHAPIAN & NEVA COYLE

FREE TO BE THIN

BETHANY HOUSE PUBLISHERS

Minneapolis, Minnesota 55438

A Division of Bethany Fellowship, Inc.

After-photos by Sue Pilon

All Scripture references are taken from the New American Standard
Bible unless otherwise noted.

Published by Bethany Fellowship, Inc.
6820 Auto Club Road, Minneapolis, Minnesota 55438

Printed in the United States of America

Library of Congress Cataloging in Publication Data

Chapian, Marie.
   Free to be thin.

Bibliography: p.
   1. Reducing—Religious aspects. 2. Christian life—
1960-   I. Coyle, Neva, 1943- . II. Title.
RM222.2.C44   1983   613.2'5   83-14126
ISBN 0-87123-560-9

This book is dedicated
to your body

Contents

Introduction

Yesterday

At 28 years old, Neva Coyle weighed 248 pounds. When people look at a "before picture" of her, they can't believe it's the same person. A hundred and thirteen pounds thinner, Neva is now an attractive, vibrant woman and the president and founder of Overeaters Victorious.

One of the happiest experiences in her life was buying a size 12 skirt and throwing out her size 24-1/2 wardrobe.

"I just wanted to be *average*," she tells her OV groups. "I used to think I'd give the world just to be average."

She remembers her many attempts to lose weight. "I tried every diet known to mankind," she says. "All the weight-loss groups and clinics, too. I'd lose weight and then gain it back, plus more."

Her motives for losing weight were varied. Maybe you will recognize some of them. She tried losing weight for her husband. She thought he deserved a slim wife, one he could be proud of. But after a while, she couldn't stick to the diet any longer. That Dairy Queen up the street was just too irresistible. Or the smell of pizza was more than she could take.

Unhappily, food had a stronger hold on her than her desire to please her husband.

She also tried to lose weight for her friends' sakes. She was singing in a church trio and the girls decided to buy matching dresses. Neva was disgraced and humiliated as they tried to squeeze her into a size 18 dress that she could barely get over her head. "I'll lose weight for them," she told herself. "Then I'll fit into one of these store-bought dresses!" (At her size, she sewed her own clothes.)

Not a strong enough motive.

It didn't work. She gained weight instead.

She dieted for special occasions: weddings, an open house, a special party or church banquet. But she never quite made it. Eating was more important than the special event, just as eating was more important than her friends and loved ones.

Being motivated to look nice is a strong motive for many people. For the overeater it is not a motive, it is a wish. Wishing something and being motivated to bring it about are two different things.

Neva, like many other overeaters, tried dieting for herself. "Do it because you like yourself," the counselors told her. The trouble was, she didn't like herself. Most obese people don't. You don't usually go out of your way for someone you don't like. And you especially aren't likely to give up something that you are passionately addicted to for someone you don't like. No, she couldn't lose weight, not even for her own self-esteem.

Desperately she sought to lose the weight but didn't know how to do it without giving up what she loved the most: eating.

Until she heard about bi-pass surgery. She went into the hospital on January 9, 1972, and had an iliojejunostomy bi-pass operation.

After this dangerous, painful and expensive surgery, she was horrified to discover that her dream of eating everything she wanted without getting fat did not come true after all. Although she lost weight initially, she soon began gaining. When she had gained 19 pounds, she panicked. She had to do something. There *had* to be help somewhere, she told herself.

Then she did something radical. Something outrageous. Something daring and fantastic. She turned to God.

Two years after the bi-pass surgery she was still suffering the after-effects of it. Worst of all, she wasn't even thin; in fact, she was still grossly overweight. She was brokenhearted, miserable and desperate.

Are you at the point of desperation yet? Are you fed up with yourself and the way you're treating your body? You don't have to be a victim of overeating any longer. You can be free!

For the eyes of the Lord move to and fro throughout the earth that He may strongly support those whose heart is completely His.—2 Chronicles 16:9

I will instruct you and teach you in the way which you should go; I will counsel you with My eye upon you.—Psalm 32:8

The Lord yearns to help you if you will permit Him. He loves you dearly. You are very important to Him and it is important to Him that you be healthy in every area of your life. He waits to help you lose weight.

Since the day back in 1973 when Neva Coyle became committed to losing weight permanently, she has lost 113 pounds and gained the attention of the world. "How did you do it?" people ask. "Will it work for me?"

Ms. Coyle appeared on CBS News when commentator Hughes Rudd and his crew flew to Minnesota to attend and film an Overeaters Victorious meeting. UPI and AP have printed stories in newspapers across the United States, Canada and Europe, telling Neva Coyle's Overeaters Victorious story. She has appeared on the Tom Snyder Show, "Tomorrow," and NBC and ABC news programs. In four years' time she went from an unhappy, obese housewife to an attractive 113-pounds-slimmer director of an international organization showing others the way to thinness and God-centered eating.

To thousands of overweight men and women, Overeaters Victorious offers hope and an answer to prayer in a dark and hopeless overeating way of life.

When Ms. Coyle cried out to God for help in her battle against overeating, she didn't imagine He would answer her own prayers in such a dramatic way, as to make her instrumental in the answered prayers of thousands of others, as well.

This book is not to promote Overeaters Victorious, but to share with you what Neva Coyle has learned and now teaches in order that you can lose weight and *keep it off*, even if you are not able to be part of the OV group meetings.

It is important to know that OV takes no credit for the success of its people, but only for the wonderful opportunity to lead people to the true and lasting answer to overeating.

This is a book about success. The people whose examples appear here were once victims of emotional disturbances and neurotic behavior. They were gorgers, "bingers," gluttons; they craved and consumed junk foods and sugar until it not only poisoned their appearance, but their personalities and health as well. They were unhappy, sick and trapped.

If you are really serious about being right with God and if you mean business about pleasing Him, living for Him and eating for Him, then He is ready to help you.

One last thing before you begin—at the end of each chapter in this book there is a prayer for you to pray. This is very important to do. Pray these prayers aloud (the more times the better). You will find a new strength and power in your life that you didn't know you could have through this victorious praying.

Now then, if you are tired of endless weight loss schemes, diets and diet clubs, and if you truly want your body, as well as your soul and spirit, in line with God's will, then this book is the book for you.

God bless you!

one

Free To Be Thin!

Carolee was 90 pounds overweight. She was lonely, angry and at the end of her rope. In her opinion, there was no answer for her weight problem. She agonized at being overweight, but continued eating and going on food binges. She and two overweight friends often went out together and did something they called "pigging out." They went from restaurant to restaurant eating until they could barely walk. The next day Carolee would suffer food hangovers worse than a liquor hangover.

Carolee went on dozens of diets. She would lose 10 pounds and gain 20; lose 5 pounds and gain 10; lose 15 pounds and gain 30. Desperate and miserable, Carolee cried out to God for help. When she found Overeaters Victorious, her small five-foot-one-inch frame weighed in at 210 pounds.

Carolee's life parallels the lives of thousands of other people who have never reached the fulfillment of their dream to be thin. Thin! Carolee tried everything she could think of to become thin—diet pills, diet shots, diet candy, diet gum, hypnosis, Weight Watchers, TOPS (she was even a national loser one year—took only 12 months to gain back what she lost plus an additional 23 pounds) and diets! She had tried them all: the Stillman diet, the Rubin diet, the grapefruit diet, the banana diet, the ice cream diet, the carbohydrate diet, the protein diet, the Air Force diet, the potato diet, the celery and carrot diet. She had taken liquid protein and lost 20 pounds. (She gained 30 pounds back and a week in the hospital.) She tried Slender Now and other powdered protein drinks and only lost 5 pounds because she'd drink the protein drink and then eat a full meal. She fasted, drank only juices for weeks at a time, and even as a last resort tried acupuncture. When that didn't work, she opted for bi-pass surgery. The surgeon told her she wasn't heavy enough. She needed to be 100 pounds overweight and she was just under that.

A person is desperate when he pursues a painful and dangerous operation such as bi-pass surgery which slices across the belly, making a 15 to 18-inch incision to disconnect approximately nine feet of the small intestine, leaving the patient with 18 inches of a functioning intestine. Side effects and complications are frequent. But still the drastic choice of bi-pass surgery is appealing—a glutton's dream. "I can eat as much as I want without gaining weight!"

Carolee, however, didn't go through with the surgery. She heard a success story that changed her life. A woman in Arden Hills, Minnesota, had lost over 100 pounds and she was helping countless others to lose weight, too.

Carolee decided to see what it was all about. She met the woman who had lost 113 pounds. "I lost every pound with Jesus," she confessed.

Carolee was very interested. "With—?"

"That's right. With Jesus," Neva Coyle told her. "Nothing else worked. Nothing. And I was pretty desperate. I mean, you're really desperate when you're willing to give up your life to be thin. And that's where I was at when I had the bi-pass surgery. Then after the surgery I started gaining again. I gained 19 pounds and the scale was going up every day! It was then that I realized overeating was a spiritual problem. And if it's a spiritual problem, the answer has to be God."

As the woman talked Carolee was captivated by the attractive blonde wearing a *belted* jacket and a skirt with *horizontal* stripes. The following week Carolee joined Overeaters Victorious, the weight-loss organization which had grown out of Neva Coyle's successful weight-loss methods.

Carolee's story hasn't ended yet. She began attending the OV meetings, doing her homework, and the Lord began to answer her prayers. Each week at weigh-in time, Carolee recorded a new weight loss. In a matter of six and one-half months, she had lost 70 pounds. Her dream of being thin was almost realized. "Like Neva, I just wanted to be *average*. I hated being called *obese*."

Then Carolee shares the most interesting part of all. "Being thin is really almost a by-product of the real victory that has happened in my life," she says. "The real victory is the one over self and self-indulgence."

Overeaters Victorious members share openly how God helped them overcome anger, fear, jealousy, loneliness, frustration through losing weight. Being thin for the first time in their lives is a dream come true, but even better is the fact that they are whole new persons.

All things are possible in Christ, and that includes losing weight.

The goal of this book is to tell you how to lose weight *forever.* If you follow the guidelines in this book, you will become thin and stay thin. You will also learn a new way of life.

Overeating isn't something that affects the body only. It is intricately involved and intertwined with the emotions. It is the personality that produces the fat, in fact. Psychologists tell us that overweight is an indication of a maladjusted personality. Overeating, especially overeating of sweets, is often a response to feelings of inadequacy, depression, anger, fear, loneliness, fear of failure, anxiety and other debilitating emotions.

Overweight people use eating as an emotional outlet. Dr. Charles S. Freed, an authority on obesity, explains, "Anything that increases the overeater's emotional tension (such as sorrow, anxiety, nervousness or irritability) increases their desire for food." [1]

Every successful Overeaters Victorious person will tell you how much *more* God did in his life than just remove extra poundage.

If you're really serious about being right with God and if you mean business about pleasing Him and living for Him, now is the time to start.

For far too long Christians have been making excuses for destroying their bodies.

Being 10, 50 or 100 pounds overweight is far more harmful than you may realize.

Dr. Frederick J. Stare[2] of Harvard University's Nutrition Department says that even ten pounds over normal weight can mean that you run the risk of dying five or ten years sooner than you otherwise might. He says ten pounds overweight is being in the "alarm zone!"

Gorging on food wounds more than our bodies. Our souls are hurt, too. Unfortunately, it has been acceptable to be obese. If there's a drug addict or an alcoholic among the members of the church, everybody can plainly see someone with a serious problem. But the obese person, addicted to gluttony, is regarded as normal.

Is obesity normal in the eyes of the Lord? Compulsive acts without evidence of disease falls under the category of psychoneurosis. Overeating is a compulsive act. Jesus went to the cross so that His people no longer need be the victims of compulsive acts. We need to ask ourselves, then, *is overeating sin?*

"Ouch!" you say. "I've never considered my overweight *sin*! I mean, I'm free to be who I am in the Lord. He loves me just the way I am! Fat or thin, I'm His and He loves me."

What shall we say then? Are we to continue in sin that grace might increase? May it never be!—Romans 6:1-2

The overweight person may say the truth with his mouth, but he doesn't really believe he or she is totally loved. That's one of the reasons for overeating. Food takes the role of the Comforter.

The overweight person also says, "I love the Lord and I want to serve and obey Him!"

There's the key to dynamic living and power—obedience. The Bible tells us in Galatians 5:23 that evidence of the Holy Spirit's working in our lives is self-control. Obeying the Lord means hearing Him when He says, "Don't eat that!" and then obeying.

Would we rather overeat than allow the Holy Spirit to hold the reins of our appetites?

Lust for food will never be satisfied. Unbridled lust is sinful, and lust for food is as sinful as unbridled physical lust for someone's body. Eating to gain a false sense of security is a false motive because only God gives us true security and safety.

Our first step, then, toward getting thin and staying thin is to consider the commitment before us. It's a wonderful and powerful commitment, one that will have a dynamic effect on us for the rest of our lives.

Are you ready?

1. Kordel, Lelord, *Eat and Grow Slender*. (Manor Books, Inc.) 1962.
2. Ibid.

two

Making a Commitment

The Holy Spirit longs to be the guiding force in your life, longs to fill every need you have.

Ask yourself this question: "Will I allow the Holy Spirit to take over my eating habits?"

If you have answered "Yes," you're ready to begin.

You are now about to learn how to bring your body into control by training your flesh in the power of the Holy Spirit.

Don't be afraid. With God you won't fail. In the past you may have failed at losing weight; in fact, you may have even failed when you tried losing weight with the Lord. Remember, God is a patient and forgiving God. He is right beside you at this moment—ready to begin work with you on your eating habits.

How Much Do You Eat?

If you are eating more than your body requires, you are putting more into it than God intended it to hold. If you are hungry for more than your body needs, it's not food you're hungering for.

We are made of body, soul and spirit. In order to be rightly aligned with the will of God, your *spirit* should be the controlling force in your life. Your human spirit, indwelled and empowered by the Holy Spirit of God, then is able to be in constant communion with God. You are able to hear His voice, understand His Word, obey Him in all things. Your body and your soul respond to the power of God in your spirit.

If your *body* tells your soul and spirit what to do, you're out of order and you will fail.

If your *soul* is in control, and this is the area most of the world is led by, you are also out of the will of God. Your soul is comprised of intellect, emotion and will. If your emotions lead your life, you are in a sorry way, vulnerable to any circumstance or event. If your intellect alone guides your life, you are without the wisdom of God who is all wisdom. If your will directs you, you are at best, stubborn.

When you are filled with food and still hungry, you are receiving some very direct signals that your inner being is longing for more than food. Filling your stomach will not satisfy that longing and the more you eat, the fatter and hungrier you'll be. The person who says, "I don't eat out of deep needs. I eat because I enjoy food," is really saying, "I don't want God to tamper with my appetite." That person may just be refusing to discipline his/her eating habits or exercise the godly fruit of self-control.

God's Promise for Success

Just before God gave Moses the law, He showed him the importance of a covenant. It was important in order to be successful, or to prosper. *Prosper* means to be successful, to thrive. (It is the overweight person's goal to *prosper* in his/her efforts to lose weight!)

God promised prosperity or success for keeping a covenant.

So keep the words of this covenant to do them, that you may prosper in all that you do.—Deuteronomy 29:9

You enter into a covenant with God to lose weight His way. You know all too well that your own ways to lose weight will bring failure and disappointment. But God will not disappoint you. Be assured that God is joining *with* you. A covenant is something requiring more than one. God will not only encourage you on your way to thinness, He will also show you the way!

You stand today . . . before the Lord, your God . . . that you may enter into the covenant with the Lord your God, and into His oath which the Lord your God is making with you today, in order that He may establish you today as His people and that He may be your God, just as He spoke to you and as He swore to your fathers, to Abraham, Isaac, and Jacob.—Deuteronomy 29:10, 12, 13

The Commitment

Before you begin to lose weight, carefully and prayerfully make your decision to commit yourself wholly to doing it *God's* way. When you come to Him on His terms, seeking His ways, asking His guidance, He will guide, comfort, encourage, strengthen and see to it you're successful.

> *For this commandment which I command you today is not too difficult for you, nor is it out of reach.*—Deuteronomy 30:11

You agree *with* Him to go on a definite retraining program. You agree *with* Him to see it through, to remain faithful. You commit yourself to either attending your OV group faithfully, doing your correspondence work faithfully, or staying on the program by yourself faithfully. Notice we use the word *faithful* but we do not use the word *diet*. Overeaters Victorious do not learn how to diet. We learn how to *eat*. Every overweight person already knows how to diet and probably knows a hundred various diets. We are not dieting; we are training our eating habits through the power of the Holy Spirit and the Word of God.

> *But the word is very near you, in your mouth and in your heart, that you may observe it.*—Deuteronomy 30:14

You can be faithful to Him and to His Word if you will connect your will to His. He has a great purpose for your life and His purpose always requires obedience on your part. In order to be obedient you have to be faithful.

> *See, I have set before you today life and prosperity, and death and adversity; in that I command you today to love the Lord your God, to walk in His ways, and to keep His commandments and His statutes and His judgments, that you may live and multiply, and that the Lord your God may bless you in the land where you are entering to possess it.*—Deuteronomy 30:15

God promises you that you will be blessed if you will listen to Him, walk His ways and keep His commandments. (Those commandments may come in the form of a loud inner voice, "Don't eat that!" while you're reaching for the cookie jar.)

You lose the promise by turning away, by choosing not to obey Him.

> *But if your heart turns away and you will not obey, but are drawn away and worship other gods and serve them, I declare to you today that you shall surely perish. You shall not prolong your days in the land where you are crossing the Jordan to enter and possess it.*—Deuteronomy 30:17, 18

Think of your "promised land" as a thin body. You can enter

into your promised land and enjoy the fullness of life that God gives to those who are obedient, or you can forfeit it.

> . . . I have set before you life and death, the blessing and the curse. So choose life in order that you may live, you and your descendants.—Deuteronomy 30:19

How do we choose life? He gives some specific directions in the next verse (Deut 30:20):

> By loving the Lord your God, by obeying His voice, and by holding fast to Him; for this is your life and the length of your days.

The Lord urges you to choose life. The choice, now, is yours.

If you don't have an intimate, personal relationship with Jesus Christ, you can. Give your life to Him, making Him the Lord of your life. He came to this world as the Son of God, to die on the cross, so that you and I could be forgiven of all sins and live a life of victory over negative and destructive forces. When He is your Lord and Savior, you have the Holy Spirit of God dwelling within your spirit to link your life with the power of heaven and eternity. It is the Holy Spirit who guides, instructs, comforts and helps you as you lose weight.

What Does Commitment Really Mean?

What does the word *commitment* mean to you? Two definitions of the word are "a pledge" or "the state of being bound emotionally or intellectually to some course of action." In order to live a dynamic Christian life in God, you need commitment. It's not something to take lightly.

If you are willing to put the Lord Jesus in the position of lordship over every area of your life, including what you eat, you must commit yourself to this idea.

Make a covenant with the Lord today regarding total commitment to Him and His will. Then make a commitment regarding losing weight. A covenant is a *binding agreement*, and your commitment to the Lord requires this covenant.

You are agreeing and binding yourself to the Lord, not to Overeaters Victorious. The overall objectives of OV are to glorify and lift up Jesus by sharing how to eat in obedience to the Holy Spirit. Your commitment is to Jesus. Your covenant, or binding agreement, is with Him.

Your commitment to losing weight and getting your body into right order is important. If your commitment is sincere, you will succeed. God promises you that. *So keep the words of this covenant to do them, that you may prosper in all that you do.*

How to Pray

Your life will take on new dimensions in strength as you continually communicate with the Lord. At the end of each chapter in this book there will be a prayer for you to pray. Pray these aloud and as many times as possible. It's important to hear yourself say these words and to concentrate on what you're saying. That's why it helps to repeat the prayer.

For example, when you say the words, "I choose," you are making a mighty spiritual stand. History has been altered with such words! When you pray these words, you are setting yourself on the right road to a thinner, happier you.

Prayer

Father, in the name of Jesus, I make Jesus the Lord of my life. I give my body, soul and spirit to you now. I receive Jesus as my Savior and I choose to live my life now by the power of the Holy Spirit.

I make a commitment to you, Lord, regarding my eating habits. I choose to put you in the position of lordship over every area of my life, particularly in the area of eating.

I choose to love you, to obey your voice and to hold fast to you because you have said this is my life and the length of my days. I choose the blessing of obedience.

In Jesus' name, Amen.

three

What Are Your Motives?

Terry S. bubbles with excitement as she tells her girlfriends about her new relationship with her mother-in-law. "We've hated each other for years!" she explains. "Now, what do you think has happened? She told my husband that since I've lost weight, the change in me has been miraculous!"

The other women nod their heads in understanding. "And how do you feel about your mother-in-law now?"

"I feel closer to her, somehow. Maybe one day I'll really love her. She's so much nicer to me now."

Terry realizes that the cause for the poor relationship was due more to herself than her mother-in-law. Overeaters are often selfish people who look at self-denial as punishment rather than a healthy response to the love of God. Terry succeeded in losing 60 pounds on the OV program, and in the process, learned a great deal about herself. "I never realized what a self-centered person I was!" she confessed. "I ate out of anger, frustration and even jealousy. I blamed my problems on everyone else." She realized that she hated sharing her husband with his mother and resented her role in their lives, something she would never have admitted to herself before.

If Terry's motives for losing weight had been selfish, she would have fed one of the strong motives that caused her to overeat in the first place. That's why her previous attempts had always failed. She had been on dozens of diets before and always gained back the weight she lost. This time she made a firm decision after she committed herself to the task of losing weight (see previous chapter on Commitment). Her decision to lose weight was to *please the Lord.*

> *We have as our ambition, whether at home or absent, to be pleasing to Him.*—2 Corinthians 5:9

A motive is the reason we perform behavior or action. As a

Christian, our motives are to be based on the Word of God. There are some strong words regarding motives in the Bible. If our motives are for earthly gains or rewards, we will not be pleasing to the Lord and therefore not benefit by His blessings. Listen to what it says in Philippians 3:18 and 19:

> *For many walk, of whom I often told you, and now tell you even weeping, that they are enemies of the cross of Christ, whose end is destruction, whose god is their appetite, and whose glory is in their shame, who set their minds on earthly things. . . .*

And 2 Corinthians 5:10:

> *We must all appear before the judgment seat of Christ, that each one may be recompensed for his deeds in the body, according to what he has done, whether good or bad, [considering what his purpose and motive have been, and what he has achieved, been busy with and given himself and his attention to accomplishing]* (brackets Amplified Bible).

These "enemies of the cross of Christ" may not be heathens, but Christians. Did you know that it's possible to be a Christian and still miss your own potential?

The Lord is not exactly pampering us here, is He? He is saying the end is destruction when our god is our appetite, when our glory is our shame, when our minds are set on earthly things. He is not saying, "If you want to eat a dozen doughnuts, dearie, you go right ahead. I understand. When you finish those, why don't you have a half gallon of ice cream? Then you can fall on the sofa, sick and miserable, and watch TV. Sure, go right ahead."

No, that's not the Lord. The Lord is telling you,

> *Delight yourself in Me. I shall fulfill the desires of thine heart.—*
> Psalm 37:41, paraphrased.

He is telling you to put aside all appearance of evil. He is saying, "Cleave unto *Me*."

Did you know that you stifle God's working in your life when you habitually overeat? He is telling us that we're proud of things we should be ashamed of.

How many Sunday school picnics have you gone on where you heaped your paper plate so high with food, you could hardly get it back to your seat without losing some of it along the way? How many potluck dinners, banquets, showers, weddings and graduations have you attended where you have joked about who could eat the *most*?

Ask yourself this question: Is it more pleasing to the Lord to exercise self-control or to eat anything, in whatever quantity *you* want?

"But I'm free from bondage!" you may protest. "I'm free from the law. Jesus has set me free. Let no man be a judge of what I eat or don't eat. I'm free in Christ and I'll eat what I want. If I'm fat, so what? Jesus loves me and is not a respecter of persons."

Now if that's what you're saying and believing, stay with us just a little bit longer. There are some real blessings in store for you. Self-control is not bondage; it's *freedom*. You are in charge of your life. Self-control is freedom! It frees you to be the real you.

- You use food. Food does not use you.
- You use calories. Calories do not use you.
- You are in control over what goes into your body.
- You are *free* from binging, gluttony and overeating.
- You are healthier, more energetic and in *control* of your life.
- You are no longer selfishly indulging in food.
- You are turning to God for your needs and desires to be fulfilled.

When your motives to please the Lord are clear and strong, you can be assured you will lose weight. God works from the inside out. Once your motives are in the proper place within your heart, you will begin to see results on the outside.

It is God who is at work in you . . . for His good pleasure.—
Philippians 2:13

Jesus did not come to earth to do any old thing He pleased. He came and lived in perfect obedience to His Father.

*And being found in appearance as a man, He humbled Himself by becoming obedient to the point of death, even death on a cross. Therefore also God highly exalted Him, and bestowed on Him the name which is above every name.—*Philippians 2:8-9

He became a model for us, showing us how to choose right motivation.

For it is God who is at work in you, both to will and to work for His good pleasure.—Philippians 2:13

He wants to perform His perfect will in you and your life. He wants to fulfill His purpose for your life. You can lose pounds and be at the weight God intended you to be. Your motive is *to please Him*. He's not punishing you by taking food away from you. He is *blessing* you and lovingly showing you how to walk in the power of His Spirit.

Happily Motivated

"Do all things without grumbling or disputing," He tells us, "that you may prove yourselves to be blameless and innocent, children of God above reproach in the midst of a crooked and perverse generation, among whom you appear as lights in the world" (Phil. 2:14-15).

That's you and I—blameless and innocent and above reproach in the midst of an overeating and junk-food-laden generation!

Sometimes it's difficult to stop complaining about the number of calories in pecan pie or how everything good to eat is fattening. But when our motives are to please the Lord, we have the power within us to *rejoice* in eating for His glory. This power is there waiting to be unleashed.

Our motives for losing weight in the past may have been selfish. Maybe we wanted to be gorgeous for some person or some group of people. Mary R. lost 15 pounds for her high school reunion. She wanted to look smashing in front of all her old classmates. She wanted to look as young as she was in high school, and she wanted to show up several of the other more popular girls who were now fat and dowdy. Two months after the reunion she had gained back the 15 pounds plus 5 more.

Do nothing from selfishness or empty conceit.—Philippians 2:3a

There is nothing wrong with wanting to look attractive. God wants us to be attractive. In fact, when a person becomes a Christian, he usually gains a new attractiveness and vibrancy. The life within gives a glow and a radiance that wasn't there before.

The Holy Spirit gives new motivation to the Christian to be attractive. When selfish and vain motives creep in, the natural working of the Lord is hindered.

God wants to make you beautiful. He will help you be—if you let Him.

Prayer

Lord Jesus, I choose now to lose weight for your sake. I give up the old motives which have in the past failed. I choose now to eat to glorify you. I will lose weight to please you. Show me, Lord, what your will is for my body. In Jesus' name, Amen.

four

Making Goals

Lois M. was always proud of the fact that she could eat whatever she wanted without gaining weight. Her friends ate salads while she ate rich desserts. They were the ones with the weight problems; she remained slim and trim. But one day she began to gain weight. Her clothes were too tight for her to wear. Zippers bulged, buttons popped. She had only 15 pounds to lose, but it could have been a hundred. It meant disciplining her eating habits and this was as foreign to her as moon travel.

Lois didn't wear her indulgences as some of her grossly overweight friends did, but she realized she had a problem that needed facing. "I had never been aware that my overeating was a spiritual *problem* until I gained so much weight I couldn't fit into my clothes," she told her OV group.

"Now, with the Lord's help, I am learning how to eat. It is really hard for me because I'm just not accustomed to saying no to myself."

In Lois' group there were women who needed to lose 50, 60 and 100 pounds. Her 15 pounds seemed like feathers next to these women's extra weight. But Lois knew that if she didn't give the Lord control over her appetite now, her problem would only get worse.

How to Find Out How Much You Should Weigh

How many times have you told yourself you want to lose so many pounds by such-and-such a day? How often have you said that you want to weigh a certain weight because you weighed that at one time and you want to weigh that again?

Before determining your goals, stop and pray about it. Ask the Lord how much He wants you to weigh. Does that sound strange to you? One woman who had been on many diets in her lifetime and was still overweight found asking the Lord how much she should weigh a phenomenon. "I just never thought of it before," she said. "I prayed. I always prayed, I mean, but I just never thought of asking *Him* how much *He* wanted me to weigh."

When this woman did pray and ask the Lord to show her how much she should weigh, she found His answer was different from her own plans for herself. She had set up high goals for herself, but she could never attain them. On the few occasions she did reach the goals she set for herself, she gained the weight back within a short period of time.

"I always tried to get my weight down to 110 pounds. But when I prayed, the Lord showed me He wanted me to weigh 125! Well, that was sure a relief. I used to have a million fears about keeping my weight at 110 pounds. I was afraid I'd have to starve to death to stay at that weight."

How do you hear the Lord's voice? You ask and then you listen. It's amazing how many Christians have never heard the Lord speak to them. I don't mean in an audible voice. I mean hearing Him deep within your own spirit. Ask the Lord how much you should weigh. When you're reasonably sure you have heard an answer from within your own spirit, pray about it. Then pray with friends. It's important you pray with understanding friends, or friends who are also losing weight. Your mother or your wife or husband may not be the right one to consult. Your mother may love you pudgy (she'd love you if you had two heads and the plague, also) and your husband may say you're fine the way you are (he just has "more to love," right?) Baloney.

Ask people who are not personally involved with you. Ask them to pray with you. Tell them what you think the Lord is telling you and ask them how that sounds to their Christian ears.

A woman in a Minneapolis OV group prayed about how much she should weigh. She heard the Lord telling her 117 pounds. She was delighted to think she would one day weigh 117 pounds. She asked her prayer partners in OV to pray with her. Before they prayed, she told them the weight she thought the Lord was giving her as a goal. "Oh, no," said one friend. "That's far too little. You don't want to weigh 117 pounds. You'll be skin and bones."

"You're large framed!" said the other. "You'll need to weigh more than 117 pounds."

(Don't believe it if you tell yourself you're "large framed."

Even if you're eight feet tall with 50-inch shoulders, consider yourself average. One woman who lost 100 pounds was shocked to discover she was actually a tiny person. You probably are, too!)

"117 pounds. Are you *sure* it's the Lord who is telling you to weigh that?"

After more of the same discouraging discussion, the women prayed. After praying, each one told the woman she was right. The Lord showed them the same—117 pounds. She is nearly at her goal as this book is being written.

So the first thing you do on your new weight-loss program is to ask the Lord how much *He* wants you to weigh.

After you ask the Lord how much you should weigh, you ask Him how many calories you should be eating a day in order to reach that goal.

Sometimes people aren't sure what it means to hear the Lord speak. Here is a conversation between two Christians. One of them, a young man of 30, has recently lost 40 pounds. His friend is a young woman who would *like* to lose 40 pounds. They are standing at the copy machine in the office where they both work.

HE: I had the most wonderful experience in the cafeteria at lunch today.

SHE: Oh? What was that?

HE: I wanted to eat a fattening dish—it was spareribs soaked in greasy tomato sauce. Ugh! Anyhow, just as I was about to order it, the Lord spoke to me and said, "Don't eat that."

SHE: What? What did you say?

HE: I said, I wanted to eat a fattening dish, spareribs soaked in—

SHE: No, no—I understood that part. It's the other part I didn't quite catch. *Who* said *what*?

HE: The *Lord* said, "Don't eat that."

SHE: That's what I thought you said. You're telling me that *God* speaks to you?

HE: Yes, He certainly does. Especially about food, now that I'm committed to this new eating program to lose weight.

SHE: You mean you hear voices?

HE: Not quite. It's not a *voice* voice I hear. It's like an inner knowing—

SHE: First sign of schizophrenia—hearing voices.

HE: I assure you I'm not schizophrenic.

SHE: What are the kinds of things God says to you?

HE: He tells me how many calories I should eat each day in order to reach the weight He wants me at. He tells me what I should be eating within that calorie limit.

SHE: The Lord tells you all that?

HE: He certainly does. He'd talk to you in the same way if you wanted Him to.

SHE: But I'm not a big religious person or anything like that.

HE: Neither am I. I'm a simple believer. That makes me His child and He talks to His children.
(PAUSE. She looks long and incredulously at her thin friend.)

SHE: Does God actually go around *talking* to people?

HE: (Smiling) He talks to His *own* people. I know that. His own people hear His voice and He knows them and they follow Him.

SHE: Yes, I believe that. But how does He *talk* to you?

HE: It's an inner knowing. It's hearing His will through His voice deep within your soul.

SHE: In words?

HE: Yes, exactly.

SHE: (Setting the dial on the copy machine) What kind of voice does He have?

HE: He speaks through my own voice and my own thoughts. I'm the vessel He uses to speak to me. Naturally, He speaks through others and through His Word, but He also speaks to me directly. How many more copies will you be making?

SHE: (Not acknowledging his question) Is it something like having a conscience?

HE: Oh, yes. He will urge you not to sin and guide you into truth. But He says more. Your conscience doesn't tell you, "I love you" or "Well done, good and faithful servant." Uh, I only need one copy of this notice . . .

SHE: (Not hearing) If I'm a Christian, I believe that God directs my decisions. He guides me and helps me in everything. Why is this different than "hearing His voice"?

HE: One is a bit more intimate than the other.

SHE: (Stacking papers, flipping lid and putting another sheet in copier) What can I do so He'll talk to *me* too?

HE: Start by asking Him questions and then listen for His answers.

SHE: Easy as that?

HE: (Helping her stack papers) You know, I read the book of Proverbs where it says, "Hear the instruction of a father, and give attention that you may gain understanding," and I repeated those words right back to the Lord. I said, "Lord, you have said right here in the fourth chapter of Proverbs to hear instruction. Well, I'm listening. Please teach me."

SHE: But He does that through His Word, the Bible.

HE: Yes, you're right. That is our foundation and it must always be the first word in all we do, think, act and say.

SHE: I just can't imagine Him telling me what to *eat*, though. That seems so small, so insignificant. How many copies will you need to make?

HE: Only one of this notice. Eating is not an insignificant matter to me! Being overweight has been a hassle for me most of my life. It's affected my Christian life, too. I've been a compulsive eater, rebellious and self-willed. God is now helping me change.

SHE: You're looking terrific. I can see a real change in you. Here, let me make that copy for you. Is it a notice telling us not to loiter at the copy machine?
(He hands her the notice.)

HE: (Laughing and reading aloud) "Smile, God Loves You And Wants to Talk to You."

To many of us the idea of God speaking to us is somehow far-fetched, weird or too good to be true. He's only supposed to talk to a few select privileged ones, certainly not *me*! When Neva Coyle was interviewed by a reporter from the *Chicago Daily News* for a New Year's article, she happily told him, "I ask the Lord what I'm supposed to eat and He tells me."

"Are you going to tell me that God *speaks* to you?" the reporter asked, a slight snicker on his lips.

Neva answered, "Are you going to tell me that water goes over Niagara Falls?"

"I don't see what that has to do with my question," the reporter answered. "Water going over a falls is a natural event. A course of nature."

Neva smiled and said, "It's a natural event for God to speak to us, too."

"But surely He doesn't speak to just anybody!"

"But He does. God speaks to everybody. It's just that many people don't listen."

It is important on the OV weight-loss program that you learn to hear the Lord speaking directly to you. However you hear His voice, whether it's an inner knowing, a direct word or a blast of trumpets in the night, you must get to know Him and get to know what He's telling you.

Overeaters Victorious differs from other weight-loss programs. Most doctors and clinics will give you sheaves of paper with menus, diets, lists of can't have's and can have's. This gives you only one responsibility and that is to buy the food you're told to buy and eat it exclusive of all else. In effect, the overweight person becomes a servant of the weight-loss program.

If you are not ill or on a special diet for health purposes, you can have your own tailor-made diet right from the kitchen of heaven.

This book won't tell you how many calories you are to eat and what you are to put on your plate at each meal. *You* get those instructions from your Lord. He's the one who formed your body (He knoweth your frame), and He's the One who wants to live in it with you. He loves you more than anybody in the whole world and is more concerned with your weight than anyone else you know. Let Him speak to you and direct *every morsel you eat.*

Please, if you're on a special diet ordered by your doctor for your health, or if you are taking special medication, do not change what you are doing without discussing it with your doctor.

A good "test" of the Word of the Lord, in fact, would be to check with your doctor and ask him if your calorie intake and goal weight sounds reasonable. The Lord isn't going to give you any instructions that are unwise, harmful to your health or unreasonable for you to accomplish. Your doctor's response should confirm this.

Hearing God's Voice

This story was told by Jeanie, despairing new OV member who had struggled with her weight for twenty-two years.

"Lunch time has always been the worst time of day for me. The kids are in school, my husband is at work and I'm alone. I can have really good intentions and put a cottage cheese salad on the table, but then something happens to me and I become a monster. I eat everything in sight. I'll stuff myself until dinner when I can hardly eat a thing. My husband wonders how come I'm fat when I don't eat anything. He doesn't see me stuffing myself all day. And he doesn't see me after everyone else has finished eating when I'm doing the dishes and cleaning up.

"I've tried a lot of things, like having the kids clean up the dinner dishes or getting out of the house during the day, but nothing lasts. I always go back to my old habits."

After completing the six orientation lessons, Jeanie wrote on her response sheet these glowing words:

"Early in the orientation when I was praying for the Lord to speak to me, a wonderful thing happened to me. I had just finished a very SMALL lunch of soup, salad and a sandwich (for me, that's small. I usually ate six sandwiches just as starters). Right then I heard the Lord say to me, very clearly and distinctly, *'Now feast on me.'*

"I got my Bible out and began to read immediately. Now every day I have lunch with my Bible open right in front of me so that when I finish the last bite, I begin to read the Word. It works! You can see by my chart I've lost ten pounds. PTL! PTL! PTL!"

Five months later, Jeanie was asked to share with others at an OV weekend retreat on beautiful Lake Independence in Minnesota. "I feel like a new person!" she bubbled. "I've lost 34 pounds and I am almost at my goal weight. When God told me to feast on *Him* instead of the food, it was like a bomb exploding in my life. I have read more of the Bible and memorized more scripture in these past five months than I have in my entire fifteen years as a Christian."

When the Lord begins to speak to you and you begin to obey His voice, you'll find yourself feeling and acting like a new person, too.

Let your words and attitude be as the young boy Samuel's when the Lord gained his attention. "Speak, Lord, your servant is listening!" (1 Sam. 3:1-18).

At the bottom of one of her lesson response sheets, an OV member wrote this moving simple prayer:

"Dear Lord, teach me. Open my ears to your truth. Grant me the grace to obey. Oh, Lord, let me know your plan for me from day to day. Love, Marla."

You are not alone in the battle against overeating. There are hundreds (thousands) of Jeanies and Marlas who are praying similar prayers right now. And God is answering in their lives. He'll answer in yours. Don't be afraid to hope in God. In obedience to His Word and His voice, your hopes of losing those pounds will become a reality.

Don't despair any longer. God is moving on your behalf. You *will* make it this time.

God promises success and prosperity in response to your obedience. Won't you right now take a moment to ask Him to speak to you?

Whether it's an inner knowing, a clear and precise thought or words formed in your own mouth, you *will* hear His will made clear to you if you listen carefully.

And do not be conformed to this world, but be transformed by the renewing of your mind, that you may prove what the will of God is, that which is good and acceptable and perfect.—Romans 12:2

"Test the spirits," the Word tells us. So you can "test" the word you receive by sharing it with others, carefully weighing it with the knowledge you have regarding nutrition and your own general health, and prayer.

If you think the Lord is telling you to go on a fad diet of, say, only grapefruit and eggs for a certain time (or some equally unhealthy scheme), please pray again. God's ways aren't faddy—they're eternal and everlasting.

Your goal is not only to lose weight, but also to learn a fabulous lifetime pattern of new eating and living. You could eat sticks for a month and lose lots of weight, but you would also probably destroy your stomach. God doesn't want any part of you destroyed. He wants you beautifully built up and adorned in His Holy Spirit, powerful and lovely in His strength and glory.

Prayer

Father, in the name of Jesus, I need specific guidance and direction in my life right now regarding my eating habits. You can see I need your help in losing the extra pounds on my body. Show me your will. Please speak to me and show me how much weight you want me to lose, how much you want me to weigh, and how many calories I need to eat each day. Speak, Lord, your servant is listening. In Jesus' name, Amen.

five

On Your Way to a Thinner You!

You have given your appetite and your eating habits to the Lord. You are on your way to an entirely new way of eating and living. You are on your way to a thinner you!

> *Do you not know that you are a temple of God, and that the Spirit of God dwells in you?*—1 Corinthians 3:16

The Lord Jesus and the Word of God are directing your motives for losing weight. You will not only lose weight, you will also make your body (your temple) stronger and healthier. What a wonderful temple for the Holy Spirit to dwell in! A strong, firm and healthy temple, not overfed, undernourished, flabby and sickly.

> *If any man destroys the temple of God, God will destroy him, for the temple of God is holy, and that is what you are.*—1 Corinthians 3:17

You will be feeding strength and vigor into your body. Instead of the overfed and undernourished body you've been accustomed to, you will be lighter, fresher and more energetic.

One woman who was at least 50 pounds overweight, possibly more, tells how she was afraid to lose weight. "I'll need the extra weight in case I get sick," she said. If you have that notion anywhere in the back of your mind, you can remove it now. Overweight hinders health; it does not help it.

At a conference on obesity and the American public held at the National Institute of Health, biochemists, physicians, psychologists and sociologists came up with a number of findings that you will want to know.

1. Men under the age of 39 who have been fat all their lives seem to have a higher cardiovascular disease and diabetes risk.

2. A 200-pound, 35-year-old man who should weigh 160 raises his risk of dying suddenly 67 percent.

3. Obesity in adulthood is associated with diabetes, heart disease, high blood pressure, gall bladder disease and cancer of the uterus.

4. Obese males have a high risk of sudden death. (Although the risk of dying prematurely is much greater for obese males than for obese females.)

5. Coronary heart disease would decrease 35 percent if everyone were slim.

Dr. William Kannel, director of a study on obesity, said, "Except for stopping cigarette smoking, the correction of overweight is probably the most important thing that can be done to control cardiovascular disease.

"We need a greater sense of urgency about obesity," Dr. Kannel asserted. "As we now do when a lump is discovered in the breast, something should be done immediately when a child is obese. This is a public health problem, not an individual doctor-patient problem."

Edward Lew, an actuary for the American Cancer Society, said that males aged 35 who are 20 percent above the optimal weight level are opting for a 5 1/2 year decrease in longevity.

The deep-rooted belief that fat means health is a faulty belief. In days past, to be thin meant to be hungry. Weight loss was usually associated with sickness.

Change your thinking to THIN IS HEALTHY.

We are not saying that you should be scrawny and gaunt, no. You should be a fit vessel for the Master's use. In the previous chapter you read about asking the Lord how much you should weigh. If you think He's telling you to weigh 200 pounds when you're five foot four inches tall, you had better do some more reading of the Word.

And you shall know the truth and the truth shall make you free. —John 8:32

If you think the Lord is telling you to eat fattening sweets for energy, you may want to do some more reading of the Word. God does not starve His beloved children with sugary foods that do not nourish the body. He doesn't prescribe greasy, fattening foods that actually rob you of energy. As one woman aptly asked, "If Jesus were here today, would you see Him coming out of a supermarket with 12 bags of potato chips, one for each disciple?"

When Jesus was preaching along the sea of Galilee, a great crowd of people were following Him. They were excited and awed at the signs and wonders the Lord was performing. Sick people were being healed, the lame were walking; oh, it was one of the most thrilling spectacles they had ever seen.

Then Jesus went up on a mountain and He sat down with His disciples for a bit. The Passover, the feast of the Jews, was at hand, and Jesus was concerned that the people needed to eat. As always, His concern was for the people.

He looked up and saw the hoards coming toward them. He knew they had been following Him in the heat and dust, pressing together in the great crowds, and they were hungry.

"Philip, where are we going to buy bread that these may eat?"

NOTICE: The Lord did not say, "Where are we going to buy candy bars that these may get some quick energy?"

They didn't have enough money to buy bread for such a great host of people. Then, Andrew told the Lord, "There is a boy here, who has five barley loaves, and two fish."

This pleased Jesus. "Have the people sit down," He said. They were going to have a feast. And the feast for this hungry and tired crowd was an all-you-can-eat high protein meal. Jesus took the loaves and thanked God for them. He distributed to those who were sitting down and then did the same with the fish. Everybody ate as much as they wanted and there were twelve baskets filled with pieces of the five barley loaves left over. The Lord multiplied a nutritious meal for the people.

If it's energy you want, eat protein, not sweets.

Your goal, remember, is to eat in obedience to God through the power of the Holy Spirit.

The Lord wants to help you in your walk of obedience. That help comes through being completely His. Your attitudes have to match His will for you. Your commitment to Him has to be complete, your goals His goals, your attention given completely to obeying Him, your obedience in His power.

You cannot fail when you give yourself completely to Him.

For those who are according to the flesh set their minds on the things of the flesh, but those who are according to the Spirit, the things of the Spirit.—Romans 8:5

You have prayed and given your eating habits to the Lord. You have given your life, your entire being to Him. You are totally His, surrendered to Him. Your desires, appetites, longings, dreams, ideas and thoughts are His. Your mind is set on the things of the Spirit.

For the mind set on the flesh is death, but the mind set on the Spirit is life and peace.—Romans 8:6

You will no longer turn to food when you are frustrated, nervous, worried, feeling rejected and unloved, or bored and depressed. You will turn to the Word of God, filling your mind with its power and wisdom and strength. Through the Word, concentrating on it, meditating on it and constant communion with the Lord, you find life and peace.

Because the mind set on the flesh is hostile toward God; for it does not subject itself to the law of God, for it is not even able to do so; and those who are in the flesh cannot please God.—Romans 8: 7, 8

The many times you have dieted before in your own strength, or in the flesh, are past now. Ask God's forgiveness for those fleshly attempts to lose weight. You receive God's blessings by knowing and doing His will for you. Now you are no longer deceived. You know God wants to help you lose weight. You know He loves and cares for your body and is right beside you helping and blessing you as you lose weight for His sake.

However, you are not in the flesh but in the Spirit, if indeed the Spirit of God dwells in you . . . the Spirit of Him who raised Jesus from the dead dwells in you, He who raised Christ Jesus from the dead will also give life to your mortal bodies through His Spirit who indwells you.—Romans 8:9a, 11

If the Spirit of God could raise Jesus Christ from the dead, He can surely help you lose weight! You have a powerhouse of strength within you. When you begin to tap its resources, you will soar with unreserved strength and will power.

You Are in Control

Let no one act as your judge in regard to food or drink or in respect to a festival or a new moon or a Sabbath day—things which are a mere shadow of what is to come; but the substance belongs to Christ.—Colossians 2:16, 17

This means that you are in control of your eating habits through the power of the Holy Spirit. Your best friend may say to you, "Oh, go ahead and have a piece of pie. I baked it just for you!"

If your friend really loves you, she or he will respect your desire to please the Lord and lose weight. They'll understand when you refuse the pie.

Ann M. comes from a large Italian family who loves to eat. The rich pastas and desserts put 80 extra pounds on Ann's small frame. Going home is always a trial because her mother insists she "have another helping," or "eat your dessert—I baked it just for you!" Ann has had to be assertive with her mother and tell her point-blank, "Mama, I am on a weight-loss program to please the Lord. I want to please Him by my eating habits. That is why I am saying no to another helping of lasagne and I won't have a canoli."

Her mother may be hurt, but it won't last. Feeding someone rich and fattening foods is some people's way of expressing love. If you show them that food does not mean love to you, they will learn to express their love in other ways.

Friends may tell you things like, "You—lose weight? That's crazy. You're not fat!" or, "Come on and splurge a little. It won't hurt to go off your program just this once!" It may be a temptation to listen to them and do as they suggest.

You do not have to sink to temptation! You can rise above it. You are living a *new* life of discipline and self-control. The food may be very tempting but you *don't* have to eat it.

"No," you answer, "I will not splurge. I will not eat that. Please don't ask me to fail."

Diets That Hurt

Let no one keep defrauding you of your prize by delighting in self-abasement and the worship of the angels.—Colossians 2:18a

Dieting in the flesh leads to delighting in self-abasement. When you are losing weight for the Lord and with His help and encouragement, you will not degrade yourself or your body. The reason is, you are aware of His love for you. He cares deeply for you and for the health and vitality of your physical body. You are now eating to please Him. You won't defile or hurt something that is precious to the Lord.

Your body is precious to the Lord. Here are some ways your body can be hurt. Avoid them!

1. *Fad diets.* Diets which require your eating only one kind of food such as a grapefruit diet or a banana diet or an all-protein diet are harmful and dangerous to your body.

A young woman sat sullenly in an OV meeting, her eyes glazed, staring straight ahead at the leader. The women sitting near her noticed her for two reasons. One was that she was definitely not overweight; in fact, she was underweight and looked gaunt and undernourished. Secondly, she had a distant and faraway look in her eye, as though she were in a mild daze.

After the meeting she asked to speak privately to the group leader. She told her she had recently lost 65 pounds on predigested liquid protein. But she was suffering heart tissue damage and nervous disorders. Furthermore, she was afraid to eat. She had been fat all her life and she worried that she'd gain it all back if she started eating again.

God does not hurt our bodies, damage our hearts and destroy our personalities when He *blesses* our weight-loss program. God does not fill us with fear or anxiety about eating. He beautifully and sweetly teaches us how to eat properly so that we never again will be overweight.

Dr. Philip White, director of nutrition for the American Medical Association, said more dollars are spent on "worthless cures for obesity than for all medical research combined—and America grows fatter.

"Weight loss without rehabilitation of the life-style that allowed the person to gain is fruitless," he said.

2. *Fasting for weight loss.* Going without food at all can be just as drastic for the overweight person as binging. It is an extreme just as overeating is an extreme. If you are going to fast, please fast for the purpose of prayer and intercession. For now, do not fast to lose weight. You will gain back the weight you lose and your efforts will have been in vain.

Some hospitals use the fasting method for the morbidly obese and gradually wean the person back onto a calorie-restricted eating program. There will be a large weight loss in the beginning of the program and later the weight will be lost gradually.

Obviously you will lose weight on a fast, but it may not stay off. Obese people can tolerate a prolonged fast better than thin people. During the early stages of fasting (first 4 to 14 days) weight loss is substantial, but it is primarily water loss and easily gained back.

Weight loss by fasting is greater in heavier people than thin people. During the early stages of a fast, as much protein is lost as fat, which is not desirable. This loss may result in arrest of hair growth and/or dry and scaly skin. As the fast progresses, fat loss increases more than protein loss.

There are some advantages to fasting. Although Overeaters Victorious do not fast for weight loss, there are benefits in fasting, including giving the overworked internal organs and tissues of the body a good rest and time for rehabilitation. Fasting (over six days) flushes out toxic matter and poisons from the body system. Fasting improves circulation and promotes endurance and stamina. Fasting renovates, revives and purifies the cells of the body.

There are many advantages to fasting. But if you must fast, do not do it for the purpose of weight loss. A Victorious Overeater is learning how to *eat*.

If you have died with Christ to the elementary principles of the world, why, as if you were living in the world, do you submit yourself to decrees, such as, "Do not handle, do not taste, do not touch!" . . . These are matters which have, to be sure, the appearance of wisdom in self-made religion and self-abasement and severe treatment of the body, but are of no value against fleshly indulgence.—Colossians 2:20, 21, 23

3. *Drugs, pills, candies, gums, shots, surgery, etc.,* are not the real answer. The lasting way to lose weight and keep it off is to change your eating habits. In desperation to lose weight, some choose painful and dangerous bi-pass surgery. In addition to the painful and tedious recovery, the surgery is effective for only five years. For some it doesn't last that long.

The pills, candies, diet helps, including surgery, miss the main reason people overeat: *fleshly indulgence.*

How did you get fat in the first place? Fleshly indulgence.

How did you lose weight and gain it back again? Fleshly indulgence. How do you stay fat even though you want to be thin? Fleshly indulgence. Why do you gain weight instead of losing? Fleshly indulgence.

You can't cut fleshly indulgence out with a knife. You can't remove it with a pill or a candy before meals or a powdered drink instead of a meal. You can't end its grip over your life with a shot or drugs. Eventually it will rear its head again, and you'll be fat.

Other bizarre weight-loss methods, including hypnotism, acupuncture and vomiting, will not produce lasting healthy results either. Such things *are of no value against fleshly indulgence.*

Let no one keep defrauding you of your prize by delighting in self-abasement.—Colossians 2:18a

The Lord is your judge and *you,* by the power of the Holy Spirit within you, control your responses to His directions. He will show you the foods you are to eat and how to eat them, if you will let Him.

The Lord is encouraging you and giving you strength and power.

. . . He who began a good work in you will perfect it until the day of Christ Jesus.—Philippians 1:6

He is not going to allow you to fail.

But first you must forsake the fad diets and restrictive programs you have attempted in the past, confessing their total inadequacy against fleshly indulgence. These diets, devices and promises have had "the outward appearance of wisdom, in self-made religion, and self-abasement and severe treatment of the body, but are of no value against *fleshly indulgence.*"

Prayer

Dear Jesus, I repent of fleshly indulgence. I confess that I have attempted to lose weight in the past outside of your will. Forgive me, Lord, for not taking the strength and wisdom you so freely and readily give. I know you love me dearly, Lord, and for that reason I will not hurt or debase my body. I will bless my body in the name of Jesus.

I conquer fleshly indulgence in the name of Jesus Christ. I now begin a new way of eating and living according to the Word of God and the power of the Holy Spirit. I turn from the old, useless ways to the new, bright and beautiful. My hope is in the Lord and not in diets and devices.

I hereby refuse, in the holy name of Jesus Christ, to put my trust in fad diets, fasting, pills, drugs, surgery or any other false promise. I declare myself free from these "outward appearances of wisdom."

I am now free to lose weight God's way!

In Jesus' name, Amen.

six

We Are Not Learning to Diet;
We Are Learning to Eat

Your days of dieting are over. You are now beginning a new way of eating and living. You're on your way to health and thinness.

For some people the word *calorie* is a dirty word. They don't even want to hear that word. They hate the idea of calories and hate even worse the idea of counting them. But you are going to count calories on your new weight-loss program. Overeaters Victorious say, "We use calories; they don't use us."

One OV group leader calls calories "God's little helpers." She tells her new members that "God's little helpers" are for our benefit, not our dismay. Some people seem to feel that a calorie is an enemy. They are accustomed to thinking everything delicious is loaded with calories, and counting them would be a horrendous chore, not to mention discouraging.

But when you ask God how much He wants you to weigh (see chapter four) the next thing you ask Him is, "How many calories should I eat each day?" If you're five foot three inches and you think the Lord is telling you to eat 3,000 calories a day, try praying a bit more about it. And ask your friends to pray with you.

The reason we don't advise everyone to go on the same diet of a certain fixed number of calories is that (1) each body is different, and (2) we don't learn how to diet in OV; we learn how to *eat*.

Each of us is individual, highly unique and important to the Lord. He loves each of our bodies and created them perfectly and specifically according to His perfect design and measurement. It is important for you to hear Him give you His own custom-made calorie quota.

In one OV group of 25 people, for instance, there may be 25 different calorie quotas. One woman will be eating 1,000 calories a day, another 800, another 950, and so on. Pregnant and nursing women will eat more calories than non-pregnant women.

You count calories to be intelligently in touch with what you're putting into your mouth. You will become aware of those little "nibbles"—those innocent little licks of peanut butter from the knife (100 calories), that eensy-weensy "bite" of Junior's candy bar (50 calories), that harmless other half of Junior's tuna salad sandwich (150 calories), that little "sip" of a malted milk (50 calories), just ten iddy-biddy cashews (100 calories)—you've had enough calories for a whole meal and you haven't even eaten yet!

You'll be using calories for your benefit from now on. After the Lord tells you the amount you can have, you'll be planning and carefully figuring out the best ways to "spend" them.

Your daily calorie allowance will become like dollar bills and you will be in charge of spending them wisely. If the Lord tells you that you're allowed 800 calories a day, for instance, you're not going to waste 400 precious calories on a piece of pie. You could have a delicious, vitamin-packed feast for 400 calories,[1] if you plan wisely.

What Is a Calorie?

Energy available in food is expressed by calories. They provide the energy needed for us to breathe, digest food and maintain body heat in order to fulfill the body functions that comprise our basal metabolism, or basic life processes. Age lowers the basal metabolism and that's why older people require fewer calories. You need calories to keep your body functioning and to supply you with the energy for muscular activity you do each day.

Excess calories are equal, no matter where they come from. Energy, whether coming from a piece of cake or a sirloin steak, is equal, in that *energy not used by the body is stored in the form of fat.*[2]

Overweight people often don't take time to learn about nutrition. The reason is they may not want to know that the foods they crave are bad for the body. One woman, so fat she could hardly sit in her chair, went to a luncheon and ate the most fattening foods on the menu, telling herself and others, "Oh, this isn't fattening. After all, everything in it is healthy. Meat, eggs, cream, butter—it's good for me!"

She couldn't be more wrong. The nutrients, cooked out of the food, were minimal, but the calories soared in huge quantities. The lunch she ate, held a walloping 2,000 calories and very few nutrients.

Some nutritionists suggest cutting your calorie intake by one-third to lose weight. That's okay if your doctor agrees, but you will want to use the calories you do eat to your advantage. *Any person on a weight-loss program should eat protein.* Protein feeds your appetite in the hypothalamus in your brain. It stops those urges and cravings for sweets and unhealthy foods. Be sure to spend the biggest portion of your calories on protein foods. Eat a complete protein at every meal and you'll lose weight faster, have more energy and have better muscle tone than if you starved yourself on salads only.

Your Daily Power

Every morning have a time of scripture reading and communication with the Lord. This time of communication with Him is important. A good place to begin your scripture reading is in the book of Colossians. From there you could read the other books of the New Testament, combined with the Psalms and Proverbs. Some people are addicted to drugs; you're addicted to the Lord. You must go to Him for your supply of strength for the day and for your instructions. This is vital.

Things you will need:
1. A small notebook
2. Pen or pencil
3. Bible
4. Calorie counter

Every morning after you have had your Daily Power Time, reading the Scriptures and praying, ask the Lord what you can eat for the day according to the calorie allowance He has given you. Then in your notebook make a record of this. Here is an example:

(the date)

Breakfast:	Calories:
Lunch:	
Dinner:	
Snacks:	_____Total

Eat only what you have written down for the day and no more. If you do go over what you have written, be sure to enter it and the amount of calories. This is not meant to put you in bondage, but to introduce to you the joy of having *control* over what goes into your mouth.

When you see that those six pecans you nibbled on before dinner cost you 100 calories, you will want to start controlling those urges to nibble.

Your notebook will become your journal. OV members treasure their journals; some say they will keep it for a lifetime. You will be amazed at what you learn about yourself through your journal.

The purpose of the journal. In your journal, on a separate page from the calorie sheet, write the scripture verse you read for the day and what it means to you. Begin each entry with a scrip-

ture verse and then apply it to yourself, making it personal.
One woman's entry in her journal for the day read:

> 1 Samuel 15:22: "Has the LORD as much delight in burnt offerings and sacrifices as in obeying the voice of the LORD? Behold, to obey is better than sacrifice, and to heed than the fat of rams."

> I've heard this scripture a million times, but somehow now it means more to me than ever before. I just never realized what it meant until now. I've lost two pounds this week and I am thrilled with the discipline the Lord is teaching me. How many times have I sacrificed the wrong things to the Lord and sacrificed for the wrong purpose!

> I feel so happy to be obeying Him! I write down my calories every day and I think I'm really happier in being obedient than I am in the actual weight loss. It's wonderful! I have obeyed for two days straight and I feel happier than I've felt in months.

> I'm really learning it's more important for me to obey the Lord than it is to lose the weight I'm losing. I love knowing I am obeying the Lord. I love feeling good about myself and I feel good about myself when I'm obedient.

There are some people (not you, of course) who protest the idea of keeping a journal. Here are some excuses they might use:

- Somebody else might read it and discover my secrets.
- I don't have time.
- It's too much bother.
- I don't have the privacy to do it.

Please don't allow these or any other excuses to rob you of the enormous benefits of keeping a journal. OV people carry their journals with them during the day. Women carry them in their purses along with a small-sized Bible. Men can carry them in their vest pockets, brief cases or lunch boxes.

One woman said, "I don't think I really knew myself at all until I began reading my own journal entries. I can't tell you what a revelation it has been. I'm discovering *me*!"

Fat people often dislike any kind of discipline. Fat people often don't want to give up anything, don't want to lose anything; they often can't stand rejection, and they eat to compensate for the lacks and failures in their lives. You are now waging a war against overeating and being fat. You are waging a war against

48

your own reasons for overeating. You will not be a fat person any longer when you start developing discipline and control in your life. You are fighting for the real you to emerge. That person is one who is *not* afraid of discipline.

That is why you are to:

1. Be sure you don't miss your Daily Power Time of reading the Word and praying early in the day.
2. Enter on a separate page in your notebook the calories and food you will eat for the day.
3. Record in your journal your scripture verse for the day and what it means to you. Enter your thoughts, feelings and moods, too.

Because your commitment to the Lord in losing weight is a real and wholehearted one, you *will* succeed.

Summary

Keep your journal. Try not to miss a single day. This discipline is good for you! Think of it as an honor to do it unto the Lord.

Keep a daily record of calorie intake *at each meal.* Total your daily calories to be sure you are staying within the limit the Lord gives you.

Prayer and reading the Word daily are as vital to you as breathing. You are dependent upon the Lord and His Word to fill you and strengthen you every day.

You are gaining control over food. Food will no longer control you.

But thanks be to God that though you were slaves of sin, you became obedient from the heart to that form of teaching to which you were committed.—Romans 6:17

You're free now—free to learn discipline and the freedom it will bring you.

Prayer

Thank you, Lord, for teaching me discipline. Thank you, Lord, for calories. I thank you especially, Lord, that I am now free from being a slave to calories as I once was. I am now free to use calories for my benefit. I choose to receive from you the strength I need to be faithful to my commitment to you about losing weight. I choose to receive from you the help and encouragement I need to faithfully write down the food I eat and their calorie content.

I thank you, Lord, that I am victorious in you.

I will read the Word in the strength of the Holy Spirit.

I will record calories in the strength of the Holy Spirit.

I will pray in the strength of the Holy Spirit.

I will retrain my eating habits in the strength of the Holy Spirit.

I am victorious because you are victorious!

In Jesus' name, Amen.

After you have prayed this prayer, pray it again.

---

1. A 400-calorie feast: one large piece broiled chicken without skin (100 calories), one huge vegetable salad with oil and vinegar and parmesan cheese (125 calories), one freshly baked bran muffin (100 calories), one six-ounce glass orange juice (75 calories).

2. The nutrient composition of cake and steak are not the same, however. Cake has little, if any, available nutrients. Steak contains protein, carbohydrate and fat. When counting calories don't consider a slice of cake and steak equally beneficial to your body simply because they may have the same amount of calories.

seven

Praise the Lord and Pass the Celery

You can burn up fat without wearing yourself out or starving half to death. You can eat fat-fighting foods. Many vegetables, for instance, are so low in calories that the metabolic process of digesting them takes more calories than is in the vegetable itself. Look at celery. It takes approximately twenty-five calories of energy to digest one cup of cooked celery or two stalks of raw celery. There are only ten calories in the celery itself, so by eating two stalks of celery you've burned up fifteen calories.

There are many fruits and vegetables that are fat-fighting foods. Some of them are: apples, green beans, beets, blueberries, broccoli, brussels sprouts, cabbage, cantaloupe, carrots, cauliflower, cherries, cucumbers, eggplant, grapefruit, grapes, lemons, lettuce, mushrooms, nectarines, onions, oranges, parsnips, pomegranate, raspberries, radishes, spinach, tangerines, strawberries, tomatoes, watermelon.

Your body will use more calories digesting fresh fruit, such as oranges, than if you drink only the juice.

These foods actually help you burn up body fat. They are rich in vitamins and minerals that form the fat-fighting enzymes.

Protein is also a fat-fighting food. Protein increases your metabolism so that you burn up 130 to 140 calories for each 113 calories of protein that you eat.

A mistake people make when losing weight is to cut out protein from their diet. A "dieter" eats low-calorie foods, but may tend to ignore the importance of fat-burning and energy-building protein.

On the following wrong diet, there is a distinct lack of protein. Your body needs protein at each meal to keep your blood sugar level high and prevent hunger and overeating. Your body needs protein to repair tissues and help wounds heal. Your body needs protein for skin, hair, nails, vital body chemicals, blood and all

	WRONG	RIGHT
Breakfast:	Go without or Juice and coffee	Eggs/cheese/fish or lean meat Whole grain bread or cereal Fresh fruit
Lunch:	Salad Coffee	Salad Cottage cheese/eggs/fish/ meat or poultry Fresh fruit Yogurt
Dinner:	Soup Salad Coffee	Fish/eggs/lean meat/cottage cheese/poultry or yogurt Steamed vegetables Salad Fruit

organs and soft tissues. If you eat protein at each meal, you will not be depriving your body of vitally needed energy.

Complete proteins are meat, fish, poultry, eggs, low-fat cheese, skim milk and yogurt. Additional protein foods are beans, lentils, seeds, nuts, whole grain cereals and breads, gelatin (not the sugary kind). Three ounces of broiled chicken has 20 grams of protein and so does a cup of cooked split peas. But the chicken has 115 calories and the peas have 290.

You will check in your calorie counter which proteins are lowest calorie-wise and what size portions to eat. One woman neglected to check her calorie counter for the number of calories in chicken. She thought she already knew without looking it up. She was unfortunately mistaken in thinking there were only 100 calories in half a chicken. She was eating two chickens a day and couldn't understand why she wasn't losing weight. She thought she was eating 400 calories in protein and she was actually eating 1,200! Combined with the rest of her calorie intake, she was eating more than what she would need to maintain her goal weight.

Let your eyes look directly ahead, and let your gaze be fixed straight in front of you.—Proverbs 4:25

One male OV member says, "Sometimes I feel as if I'm fighting an addiction, a physical addiction—as much as any kind of alcohol, tobacco or drug addiction. My only weapon is the Word of God. I choose to stand on the Word. The Lord says in His Word He won't forsake or leave me."

You have your goal set before you. You have purposed in your mind to succeed and you will. Be meticulous in counting your calories and planning the best way to spend your calorie dollar bills.

Shopping

Before you go shopping, arm yourself with the Word of God. Use these words as your weapon against fleshly indulgence:

> But put on the Lord Jesus Christ, and make no provision for the flesh in regard to its lusts.—Romans 13:14

Write those words at the top and on the margins of your shopping list in bold letters: MAKE NO PROVISION FOR THE FLESH. Carry them in your hand. Repeat them again and again to yourself. "Make no provision for the flesh, make no provision for the flesh, make no provision for the flesh."

You will absorb the power in those words and do your grocery shopping in the spirit instead of the flesh.

When you're armed with the Word of God, carrying it with you, repeating it to yourself, holding it in your right hand, it's going to be difficult to reach for that bag of marshmallows with your other hand.

Be sure when you go shopping that you go *after* you've eaten. Do *not* go to the grocery store hungry. And remember, any cheese samples or other sample foods cost calories. Do you want to spend your calories on free samples at the store? Your shopping list of high-protein and vitamin-mineral-packed foods is in your hand. You have your eyes set with a fixed purpose, your gaze is straight before you. You're not going to stop and browse around the bakery department. *Too expensive!* You won't spend your precious calories on bakery items. In fact, we suggest you skirt around all those departments that may be too tempting for you.

Be nice to yourself. Wheel your shopping cart along the aisles of food that God placed there just for you. The produce department with the heaps of beautiful fresh vegetables and fruits, and dairy department with the refrigerated cases filled with marvelous protein blessings such as yogurt (plain, of course), cheeses and low-fat cottage cheese. Then fill the rest of your cart with poultry, fish, eggs, meat, whole-grain cereals and breads, and you'll have a happy supply of healthy, energy-building meals to bring home.

"But if I bought those foods, my family wouldn't eat!" you may protest. Your family loves their high-calorie, low-food-value junk food, you say.

So did you at one time. That's why you're overweight today. You have been eating the wrong foods and you have been feeding the same to your family.

Here is what Barbara D. wrote on an OV response sheet:

> In the past four months I have lost 35 pounds and I am now only ten pounds away from goal. My eating habits have drastically changed. I went from a junk-foodaholic to a responsible and nutrition conscious person. In spite of this, I still found myself buying the junk food for my family! The foods I just wouldn't touch for myself I fed to them. I was really convicted about this. I felt like I was poisoning them. They ate heavy, rich foods, sweets, drank soda pop and snacked on greasy chips and other junk foods. I had to repent to the Lord for feeding my family what I couldn't have. It was like I was getting some kind of subliminal kick out of their eating what I wasn't allowed to! Now they're learning to like healthier foods!

Letter after letter arrives at the OV office from women who are discovering they are the major cause for their family's poor eating habits.

If you have a family addicted to junk foods, first of all, remember who bought most of those foods for them. Then repent, ask the Lord for forgiveness and the ability to slowly wean them onto a healthier diet. Start by making luscious fruit salads, broiled meats (skip the rich gravies and substitute natural juices) and fresh steamed vegetables. Try making healthy fruit juice drinks in your blender. For snacks, try introducing raw nuts and seeds, cheese and crackers, yogurt, fresh fruit. And instead of the sugar-packed cereals in the morning, try feeding them a high-protein breakfast of eggs, cheese, fish, whole-grain bread or toast or a whole-grain cereal with honey.

Inventory-Time for Your Cupboards

You'll be asking the Lord three things on your new weight-loss program.

1. How much does He want you to weigh?
2. What is your calorie limit to maintain a consistent weight loss?
3. Is there food in your kitchen that shouldn't be there?

This last item requires some special discipline on your part. Most fat people have a lot of food stored in the house, so this assignment will take some time and effort to do.

You will take inventory of your cupboards, taking out each can, box and package, and reading the labels. The purpose of this inventory is to learn what you are putting into your body and the bodies of your loved ones. Experience has proven fat people do not read labels, nor are they aware of the content of the foods they put into their mouths. Taste is the important thing to a fat person.

But you are losing the old "fat" ways. You are becoming healthier, thinner and *smarter*.

Be wise as a serpent the Bible tells us. *Wise* means able to reason and think. When you pick up a package of cereal and see that the first item on the ingredient list is *sugar* and there's also a list of preservatives and chemical additives, plus a heap of calories to each serving, stop and reevaluate whether or not it is wise to eat it.

Diane O. was one of the first Overeaters Victorious to take inventory of her kitchen. She divided all the food from her cupboards and spread it out on the counters. On one side she put the food she could eat and on the other side the food she couldn't eat. Then in another place she piled the food she didn't want anybody to eat.

She did the same with the food in the refrigerator and in her pantry. She used her journal-calorie log notebook to write lists of products that were nutritious as well as low in calories. The members of her family were not on a weight-loss program, so they could eat certain foods she could not. But she didn't want them eating the junk food that had filled her cupboards for so long. It would take some gradual and loving retraining on her part to wean her family off the rich, gooey desserts and the fast foods loaded with preservatives and chemical additives.

"It was a real shock to me to discover what was actually inside those boxes and cans. I learned that I was more influenced by advertising and commercials than I was by the truth. If a commercial on TV said that a food was nutritious and healthy, I went out and bought it. If an advertisement in a magazine had a picture of someone suntanned, healthy, thin and smiling next to a food product that was really junk, I'd buy it because the advertisement made it look healthy. I didn't realize what I was doing."

Diane was like thousands of Americans who listen to the actor on TV dressed in a doctor's coat telling you that a certain product is good for you. She bought the product without reading the label or finding out the real truth.

One mother said, "Sugar is addictive. I know that. I have read about refined sugar and I know that it is just like putting poison into our bodies. It is addictive and makes one's appetite scream more! more! more! more! It makes my children either hyper or slow and drunk. It makes me retain liquid. It makes me fat and makes my teeth rot. I have to ask myself, 'Can I include it as a part of my regular eating program? Can I wholly and honestly feed sugar-laden foods to my family?' I want to be victorious and wise. The responsibility is mine."

You may not think you eat much sugar, but when you take inventory of your cupboards and your refrigerator, you'll be surprised at what you discover. There's sugar in catsup, pickles, mayonnaise, soups, Jello, canned fruits, most cereals and all salad dressings. Sugar is often labeled as "carbohydrates" and this may confuse you, an unsuspecting buyer. You may also see these words on labels. They mean *sugar.*

Dextrose is a chemical sugar, derived synthetically from starch. It is also called corn sugar.

Fructose is fruit sugar.

Maltose is malt sugar.

Lactose is milk sugar.

Sucrose is refined sugar, addictive.

Glucose is a sugar found in fruits and vegetables. It is blood sugar, an essential element in the human bloodstream. Don't confuse it with the sucrose in soda pop or candy bars. They are not the same. Glucose is important for your health.

The advertisements may tell you that sugar is "100% natural," but so is rattlesnake venom. Read your labels. Know what you're buying.

Don't Plan for Failure

Sue R., after taking an inventory of her cupboards, learned that she had a habit of tucking certain fattening items away for future failures. In case there would be a day when she didn't want to stay on her weight-loss program, there was something in the cupboard to fail with, something fattening and calorie loaded.

Don't plan for failure. Plan for success! If you *plan* to succeed, you *will* succeed.

Fill your cupboards and refrigerator with foods you *can* eat. If your family eats foods that you can't, keep them where you can't see them. Don't leave cookies in see-through containers if they're tempting to you. Don't leave dishes of candy around on tables if you're tempted to eat it. Don't store the cake where you can see it (especially if it has already been cut. You may be tempted to "shave off a thin slice"—and then miserably discover you've shaved off and eaten half the cake). Besides this, clear the table when you're finished eating so you don't eat up the leftovers.

Marge D. gained five pounds one week although she rigorously stuck to her diet. She realized that nibbling on the leftovers had to be the reason. The crisp end of the roast beef, Junior's frosting from his cake, a lick of the peanut butter off the knife, the cake crumbs from the cake pan, the last of the gravy in the pan, the leftover macaroni—"just a teensy taste."

Those teensy tastes can be devastating. One tablespoon of grape jam has 50 calories; a half cup of potato salad is 175 calories; one large oatmeal cookie is 100 calories. The extra nibbling you do through the day may add up to enough calories for two meals.

You are committed to losing weight and getting your body under submission to the Holy Spirit. You are making no provision for the flesh and its lusts. You are no longer a person who has no control over what foods go into your body.

By taking an inventory of your cupboards, you will find out some interesting things about yourself, as well as learn more about the foods you buy. You may discover, as one woman shared in her group, that she had been buying candies and sweets "for her children," but she would hide them in the back of the cupboard and eat them herself. Those high-calorie foods you think you're buying for your family, children or friends have a way of never getting past you.

Perhaps you're like the woman who buys packaged pastries ("for the family," of course) and on the way home from the store in the car, she eats one, and then she eats another. She feels guilty about bringing home the pastries with two missing, so she finishes the whole package.

Or maybe you've had the same experience as the man who bought ice cream "for the family" and ate every spoonful himself.

Check your motives for buying foods. *Make no provision for the flesh.* If having ice cream in the freezer is a stumbling block for you, don't buy it.

Let your eyes look directly ahead, and let your gaze be fixed straight in front of you.—Proverbs 4:25

Remember, your goal is to be thin for the glory of God.

After you have eliminated the junk foods and high-calorie foods from your cupboards and supplied your shelves with plenty of healthy, fresh foods and filled your refrigerator with fresh vegetables and fruits, low-calorie and nutritious foods, you can stand back and take time to feel terrific. You can see you are really serious about your commitment. The fruit of your desire really *is* to please the Lord. Your desire really *is* to be thin and glorify Him in your body. It isn't just talk. You are acting on your commitment! You are free to be thin!

The average fat person goes on 1.5 diets per year and makes over 15 major attempts to lose weight between the ages of 21 and 50. Their attempts almost always fail and the next year they're back on another diet. The reason for the failure is (1) the use of drugs for weight loss, and (2) fad diets.

Millions of books on losing weight are sold each year; there's a billion-dollar business in over-the-counter pills, powdered drinks, chewing gums, rubber sweatsuits, exercise devices and a host of other items promising a thinner you. You can rejoice that you are doing more than reading a book or buying a lot of diet paraphernalia. You are acting on a commitment to the Lord.

You have taken inventory of your cupboards. You are changing your eating habits. You're terrific.

Stand fast therefore in the liberty wherewith Christ hath made us free, and be not entangled again with the yoke of bondage.— Galatians 5:1 (KJV)

You're not in bondage to food when you're in control of what you eat. Bondage is slavery. And a slave has to do everything his master tells him. The cookies in the Tupperware container can beat against the lid and call your name if they want, but you're listening to the strengthening, guiding voice of the Lord. The pastry shop and ice cream parlor can appear so inviting you can almost hear them shout "Come on and eat!" from across the street. But you're not their slave any longer. You're free. You can say NO. And at home there is nothing in your cupboards to hold you captive. You won't be prowling out of bed at 3 a.m. to eat some ugly fattening thing. You're free from that bondage. You're free to be healthy, thin and beautiful to the glory of God.

Prayer

Dear Lord, thank you that I am free to be in control of what I eat. Show me, Lord, the mistaken thinking that has held me in bondage and made me fat. Show me, Lord, the deceptions that have caused me to overeat and harm my body. I choose to be free in you. I choose to be free from the bondage to food that has caused me to be fat.

I repent, in the name of Jesus, of the deceitful eating I have done in the past. I repent of deviously buying wrong foods and telling myself they were for someone else. I repent of eating these foods.

Thank you, Lord, for the strength and direction you constantly give me. Thank you, Lord, for your great love for me. In Jesus' name, Amen.

eight

A Word to Add to Your Vocabulary: *Obedience*

Daniel, a man of God in the Old Testament, was not without his problems. Right from the beginning, he needed to make some important choices about his life-style and eating habits. He knew how God instructed His people to eat and he was dedicated to his Jewish traditions. But in the first chapter of Daniel, when Jerusalem was besieged by the Babylonians, Daniel was one of the young men taken captive to serve in the court of the foreign king, Nebuchadnezzar.

This king wanted Israeli boys who were:
1. Good looking
2. Intelligent in every branch of wisdom
3. Endowed with understanding and discerning knowledge
4. Possessed with the ability to serve in the king's court.

When these young men were taken to the court of the king, they were to be instructed in the literature and language of the Chaldeans for three years. They were to eat the king's choice food and drink the wine he drank. Then, at the end of their three-year education, these "chosen" ones were to enter the king's personal service.

Have you ever considered yourself in training for the *King of King's* personal service? Do you believe yourself to be of the "chosen" for God's service?

In the New Testament, the apostle Peter writes to "chosen ones" who are aliens in foreign places. These aliens "who are chosen according to the foreknowledge of God the Father, by the sanctifying work of the Spirit" (1 Pet. 1:1b, 2).

A Christian is an alien without going to a foreign land. We're aliens because our real home is in heaven. This is our earthly dwelling place until the day we show up on the doorstep of our real homeland, heaven.

One woman, upon studying this verse, told her group, "I'm an alien in my own body! I don't belong in this fat body! The real me ought to live in a thin body!"

The body is visible evidence of the fruit of self-control.

There's a little word in this scripture passage that overeaters don't like. It's *obedience.*

The Christian is a chosen alien, "chosen according to the fore-knowledge of God the Father, by the sanctifying work of the Spirit, that [we] may obey Jesus Christ and be sprinkled with His blood: May grace and peace be [ours] in fullest measure" (1 Pet. 1:1b, 2).

We have been chosen so that we may *obey* Jesus Christ! Then it reads, following the colon, *May grace and peace be yours in fullest measure.* You may wonder why that phrase comes after the word "obey."

When you are in obedience you have grace and peace *in fullest measure*! It's a dazzling thought.

That's the place where Daniel was. He saw all those rich, choice foods and wines of the king's and he simply said, "No." (How easy it is to form the word *no* with our lips and how difficult to say it when there are rich, fattening foods around.)

Daniel and his three friends were the only ones who refused the king's food and wine. Daniel made up his mind *that he would not defile himself* with the king's choice food or with the wine which he drank (Dan. 1:8).

Have you ever thought that your overeating was *defiling?*

Defile means to make filthy or dirty; befoul. It means to tarnish the luster of; render impure, corrupt. Further definitions are to make unclean or unfit for ceremonial use; desecrate and to violate the chastity of.

Think of the last time you binged on some rich or fattening food. By eating that food, you were actually making your body filthy, unclean, unfit, desecrated.

Alarming, isn't it?

Usually when we overeat, it's not our bodies we're thinking about. We're more intent on satisfying an emotional need. (More about causes of overeating in chapter seventeen.) When you sit down to dinner, do you think about your heart, lungs, blood pressure, or tissue and muscle needs? Probably not. You're thinking about how hungry you are and how good the food looks and smells. You couldn't care less about your vital organs or metabolism.

Smokers have similar unconcern for their bodies' needs. A male patient, aged 42, is in a hospital with cancer of the throat. It's painful and life-consuming. In spite of his body screaming for relief from cigarette smoke, he continues to puff on three packs a day. His doctor is frantic. "If you don't stop smoking, you'll die!" he pleads. The man looks him straight in the eye and says, "Then I'll die—but I'll die smoking."

For those who are according to the flesh set their minds on the things of the flesh, but those who are according to the Spirit, the things of the Spirit.—Romans 8:5

Getting Control of the Flesh

Your flesh, or selfish worldly mind, is something you can control. Uncontrolled, our flesh is wild, unruly; it kicks its heels, rears its head against anything in its way. It is selfish, unthinking, propelled by stupid, meaningless passions. Your flesh has nothing good about it *unless* it is under the dominating influence and power of the Holy Spirit.

If your fleshly mind is in control, you'll defile your body at every chance. If you're at a party and there are rich foods on the table, you'll gobble them up without a thought. You may even continue to eat when you get home. Then you may find yourself on a full-fledged gorging binge!

Your flesh is miserable, wretched; doesn't know how to make a single wise decision. It always acts *against* the will and beauty of God.

The only time the flesh is beautiful is when it is listening and obeying the Word of God. "For the mind set on the flesh is death, but the mind set on the Spirit is life and peace" (Rom 8:6).

One woman shared how she read a book on dieting in one sitting and by the time she finished the last chapter, she had eaten six chocolate bars and polished off a quart of diet soda.

Well, at least there were no calories in the soda, you may think, but the unhealthy chemicals and additives made up for the missing calories.

If our bodies had voices, the first thing they might say to us would be, "Stop putting that junk into me!" They do tell us this, in fact, not with words, but with fat, pain, disease, lack of strength and vitality, nervous disorders, headaches, sleeplessness.

One woman tells how she was killing herself with her eating habits. "And all the time I was nagging my husband about his smoking. We were both killing ourselves—he with nicotine and me with a fork and spoon."

Daniel was chosen to serve a king, Nebuchadnezzar. You and I are chosen to serve the King of Kings. Our old fleshly ways may have hurt our bodies with our undisciplined appetites, but now we choose *not* to defile our bodies. We choose *not* to eat the foods of the world, those foods our flesh defiles us with.

"Those who are in the flesh cannot please God" (Rom. 8:8). The incongruous thing about some Christians is that in church they'll worship God in spirit and truth and have a wonderful spiritual time. Then after church they'll run home and have dinner in the flesh, wolfing in all sorts of defiling foods. It seems odd to be in the spirit one minute and then, as soon as food is brought into the picture, we abandon our spiritual mind and jump right into the ways of the flesh.

> . . . the mind set on the flesh is hostile toward God; for it does not subject itself to the law of God, for it is not even able to do so.—Romans 8:7

Daniel did not abandon his spiritual mind. He refused to defile himself with the king's food, and he convinced the commander of the officials to allow him and his friends to eat vegetables and water for ten days. He told the overseer to see for himself at the end of the ten days if they were not healthier and more robust than all the youths who had been eating the king's choice food.

Naturally, they were healthier and more robust than all the others. So the overseer agreed to continue withholding the king's choice food and wine so they could *stay* on their diet. Notice, *stay*. Daniel wanted to *stay* on the diet.

He wasn't doing penance by eating only vegetables and drinking water, or doing a short-term slim-up program. He *wanted* to eat that way. He didn't consider the king's choice food to be desirable at all. He found those foods distasteful and repugnant.[1]

What do you think of when you say the word *delicious*? If you think of some rich, fattening thing, *stop*. You can change your ways of thinking. No longer consider the king's choice food as delicious. Think of those rich, fattening foods as ugly, undesirable.

Food is not meant to tantalize and torment us. Food is meant to bless us and strengthen us. It is meant to satisfy our bodily needs for nourishment. Stuffing ourselves with fattening dainties to satisfy taste buds will never satisfy the tiniest spot of fleshly appetite. Fleshly appetite always calls out hungrily, "More! More!"

You can train your mind to stop thinking of food as delicious, tantalizing, luscious, mouth-watering or any other such adjectives as long as you set your mind to losing weight. After committing yourself to Jesus instead of overeating, you must train your mind to think about winning the battle with food.

When an athlete goes into a game, he's all psyched up to win. The coach talks WIN, the cheerleaders out on the field sing and cheer WIN, the crowds in the stands shout and wave banners, WIN!

What do you tell yourself when you're out on the field fighting against fat? WIN WIN WIN? Or do you tell yourself fleshly words like, "Oh, poor me. Everybody else gets pie. I get carrots"?

There's tremendous power in your mind. God has given it to you. You have a strong will. Your will can choose the flesh or the spirit. You can blame Satan all you want for your fat, but he doesn't eat the food; you do. Satan may tempt you, but you're still the one who does the eating.

It's your *flesh* Satan appeals to. That is why it is vitally important that you reclaim your fleshly mind from his influence and put it where it belongs—under the power and influence of the Holy Spirit of God who loves you.

King Nebuchadnezzar talked with the young men and out of all the youths he had recruited, none was found like Daniel and his friends. When Daniel ate according to the wisdom of the Holy Spirit, he was rewarded not only with good looks and a healthy body, but also God's blessing of:

1. Knowledge and intelligence in every branch of literature and wisdom;
2. Understanding of all kinds of visions and dreams.

He and his three friends were ushered into the king's royal service and, once in, they proved valuable to King Nebuchadnezzar. When the king consulted them regarding matters of wisdom and understanding, he found them ten times better than all the magicians and conjurers who were in all his realm.

Their vegetarian diet was not the only reason for these young Jews' tremendous godly power, of course. Clearly, they prospered because they *obeyed* God. The diet was just the means God used to draw them into the intimacy with Him that only obedience brings!

Please say that word out loud. Say it. *Obey.* Then say *I obey.* Now please say these words out loud:

I obey the Lord.

I choose to obey the Lord.

I am a person of obedience.

Obedience is not penance.

Obedience is not punishment.

Obedience is a blessing.

I will obey the Lord.

I will not defile my body.

Disobedience defiles.

If you eat a chocolate eclair on the way home from the grocery store, it's not the eclair that disobeys. It's you.

Look at rich unhealthy foods not as fattening, but as defiling. One of the girls in an OV group said that she couldn't eat something if she found a hair in it. No matter how hungry she was, if there had been a hair in it, she couldn't touch it. Another woman felt the same way about flies or cockroaches. If she were ever to find a fly or cockroach in the food, to her it was defiled.

A woman in New York baked a layer cake in her oven. When the cake had finished baking, she opened the oven door and found a dead, cooked rat stretched across and stuck in the cake. Unknown to her, there had been a rat in the oven when she put the cake in to bake. Would you say that cake was defiled?

You wouldn't want to eat a hair, a roach, or a rat, but that eclair or those greasy french fries may be just as defiling. If you are disobeying God and eating more calories than you should be, cry out to the Lord for help. He won't turn His back on you. He is right there with you to help you. And don't ever give up. No matter how many times you stumble, get up and begin again. God loves you and doesn't give up on you.

For I am confident of this very thing, that He who began a good work in you will perfect it until the day of Christ Jesus.—Philippians 1:6

He's not going to forsake you in your hour of need. And if you stumble a little, He's not going to throw His hands in the air and give up on you. God granted Daniel favor and compassion (Dan. 1:9) when he chose to eat vegetables and water for the glory of the Lord. He'll grant you favor and compassion, too, on your new eating program, because He loves you just as much as He loved Daniel.

Prayer

Thank you, Lord Jesus, for favor and compassion in my eating habits. I have committed my eating to you, Lord, and I am committed to losing weight. I will obey you, Lord, and eat as you show me. Give me wisdom and knowledge so that I can be a blessing to others and to you.

I choose not to defile myself, as Daniel chose not to defile himself with ungodly food. I need your help and your strength, Lord. My flesh is weak. In the flesh I choose wrong things and I do not please you. But my mind set on the Spirit is life and peace. My mind set on the Spirit is *obedience* and a new body with which to praise you.

In Jesus' name, Amen.

---

1. Daniel's diet was a prolonged one and would have been a beautifully balanced one, rich in vitamins, minerals and protein. It would have included combinations of such vegetables as cabbage, onions, celery, cucumbers, lettuce, greens, tomatoes, potatoes, peas, lentils and various beans. If you decide to go on a diet like Daniel's, be sure you are eating vegetables that include all of the necessary *vitamins, minerals* and *protein* that your body requires. Remember, you need at least 45 to 60 grams of protein a day! If you decide to eat as Daniel did, be sure to know what vegetables you must eat to get the proper nutrition. Otherwise, you're going on another fad diet.

nine

Delighted and Fulfilled

Darlene L. woke up Sunday morning feeling very sorry for herself. She planned on going out to dinner with friends after church and she knew she'd have to eat a salad while her friends would be chomping away on the fattening foods she used to adore.

At church, she asked her pastor, "When will this all end? Will I always be on a diet?"

"But you aren't on a diet," he responded quickly; "you're learning how to *eat*, remember?"

"Yes, yes, but sometimes I feel like I'm on a diet. And it feels like I'll be on one forever and ever."

The pastor smiled at her and said, "You know when the Word tells us that 'He who began a good work in you will perform it until the day of Christ Jesus,' it means He'll keep working for a long, long time."

Darlene was reminded that her new way of eating was not just something to do until she peeled off the weight she wanted to lose—it was *forever*. Daniel didn't eat vegetables and water for ten days only and then binge on the king's food the eleventh day.

You are going to have to eat the Lord's way, getting your body thin and staying thin—or you'll go back to the old ways of the flesh. You remember all too well those diets and programs. You lost weight, reached your goal and then gained it all back again.

Darlene needed to discover the *joy* in her new eating habits. She was devoted to losing weight and did everything right, but she needed joy in her life.

She didn't defile her body with wrong foods.

She wrote in her journal daily.

She stuck to the calorie allowance the Lord gave her.

She carefully took inventory of her cupboards and removed every fattening and unhealthy food from them.

She steadily lost weight and on weeks when she didn't lose anything, she continued steadfastly in spite of discouragement.

But she lacked one thing: joy. Every meal was a trial for her. She watched her friends eat whatever they pleased. They were thin and she was fat. She saw the commercials on TV for rich and fattening foods and she drooled. She saw the ads in the magazines and on billboards and everything in her cried, "I want!"

This can be one of the subtle pitfalls for the overeater. Some people go on a fast and spend more time in the kitchen than when they're not fasting. They don't eat, but they touch, feel, handle and prepare food. Their delight in food is still there, even though they're abstaining. One woman prepared a picnic dinner for her family while fasting. She prepared a huge bowl of potato salad, something she always loved to eat, and several other dishes. She was very proud of herself for preparing this picnic dinner. It was one of the most elaborate meals they had ever taken on a picnic.

She didn't eat one morsel. Her husband raved at her self-control and discipline.

When her days of fasting ended, do you know what she did? She made a huge bowl of potato salad and ate the entire thing herself. It nearly killed her. She had to go to the hospital and have her stomach pumped.

It's important that we don't take inordinate *delight* in food. Did you know you can delight in it when you're not even eating it? Don't describe rich and fattening foods as "yummy" or "delicious" or "out of this world." They aren't! One disgusting food product, loaded with sugar and chemicals, calls itself "heavenly." What an insult. Heavenly food is healthy and vitalizing, not loaded with sugar, white flour, preservatives and chemicals.

Delight yourself in the Lord.—Psalm 37:4

He is our delight. Food is not our delight.

Overeaters Victorious delight in eating God's food, in obeying Him and loving Him. Our desire is to please Him. Our desire is to love Him and serve Him with our bodies, souls and minds.

Delight yourself in the Lord; and He will give you the desires of your heart.—Psalm 37:4

Are you asking God to take away an ungodly appetite? If you are, be sure you are not delighting in ungodly *thoughts* about food.

Don't lust for ungodly foods even though you're not eating them. The Lord spoke against lust in our hearts when He said that not only committing adultery was a sin, but *thinking lustful thoughts* was just as sinful.

> *But I say to you, that everyone who looks on a woman to lust for her has committed adultery with her already in his heart.*—Matthew 5:28

When you ask God to take away your ungodly appetite, He replaces it with knowledge and intelligence in the matters of food and nutrition. If you're abstaining from ugly fattening foods but still drooling over them, *stop immediately* and change that way of thinking. Your delight is in *the Lord* and in thinking *His* thoughts!

Communication with God includes the attitude of your heart as well as your words in prayer. You communicate with Him by your obedience (or disobedience) to Him. You communicate with God by the attention (or lack of attention) you give Him. God is approachable on levels other than verbal ones. Delight yourself in the Lord and your whole being will adore Him. Your whole being is then fulfilled.

"Delight yourself in the Lord and He will fulfill the desires of your heart." Who gives us our desires when we are submitted to God? God himself. It was He who gave you the desire to be thin. Your desire is *His* desire and your delight is in Him.

Darlene had her *desire* in the right place—that is, she *desired* to *please* the Lord. She *desired* to change her eating habits and eat unto the Lord, but she didn't have any *delight* in it.

Delight means a "high degree of pleasure or enjoyment; joy; rapture; great pleasure and satisfaction; to please highly."

Darlene wanted to know how to delight in the Lord with her eating. She meditated on Psalm 37:4 and the following week told her group that she was learning she only partially obeyed the Lord. She followed her calorie allowances perfectly, but she did it with a resentful heart.

"Do all things without grumblings or disputing" (Phil. 2:14) was the Bible verse she had written in her journal. "When I was young, my father was very strict with me. He was always saying no to this or that. I couldn't do the things the other kids did or go places with them. I always obeyed him, but I resented his rules. I felt deprived.

"Now I see that I was the same way with the Lord. I would do what He said to do, but I'd have no delight in it or in Him. Losing weight was just like being deprived of the good, fun things again."

Darlene is seeing how deceived she had been. She is now learning to *delight* herself in the Lord and obey Him. She sees that it's Satan who deprives us by suggesting that ugly foods are delicious and we can't have them. He influences the flesh to eat ungodly foods and consider them yummy, mouth-watering and tasty. God *gives*, restores, lifts up, builds, strengthens and blesses. Satan destroys, kills, murders, lies, deceives. God is all truth and love. Satan has no truth or love in him.

Do you know what your own true desires are? The verse we are looking at in Psalms reads, *The Lord will fulfill the desires of your heart.* Is it your desire to be thin? If it is, then ask yourself another question: Am I doing all I can to cooperate with God so that He can fulfill my heart's desire to be thin?

If your desire is to be a certain weight, you will want to cooperate with the Lord so that you don't get in the way of His fulfilling your desire. OV members keep a Desire-Action Sheet such as the one below. On one side write your desire. This desire to be thin is one that He gave you in the first place. So you write His desire as well as your own when you write your goal weight. On the other side you write what it is God is having you do or change in your life so He can bless and fulfill your desire.

Example:

You can make a Desire-Action Sheet for yourself. Write the desire of your heart that you are asking the Lord to fulfill. On the other side write how you are cooperating with Him to fulfill this desire.

Delight in your new eating program. Delight in your commitment to the Lord. Delight in your calorie allowance. Delight in self-control and obedience to the Lord!

DESIRE	ACTION
1. I desire to weigh 117 pounds.	1. I will stay within the calorie limit the Lord gives me. a. By feeding on the Word to bridge the gap between calories I eat and calories I want. b. Planning what I eat ahead of time. c. Making sure I have satisfying food in the house to eat. d. Being a wise shopper.
2. I desire to lose 30 pounds in the name of Jesus and for the glory of God.	2. Keeping my journal, so as to be in touch with myself and observe patterns and habits God is changing and breaking.

Barbara B. said that although she has lost 60 pounds as an Overeater Victorious, her real joy was not in the weight loss, but in her obedience. "I really *delight* in the Lord," she told a group of new members. "I have to tell you that through losing this weight, what the Lord did in my heart and life is far greater than the weight loss. I am new through and through."

Delight yourself in counting calories. It is not drudgery or a hindrance! It is your freedom and your blessing. Thank God for calorie counters! Thank God you can lose weight for Jesus! Thank God He is fulfilling the desires of your heart because your desires are His desires. That's how close you are to Him. You are special and dear to Him. You eat in the Spirit now, not in the flesh.

Make a Desire-Action Sheet for each week. What can I do this *week*? Keep it in your journal and refer to it as the week progresses. The reason for this is that you could write on the desire side, "To lose ten pounds," and then a year later, you're still ten pounds overweight. Your desires *work together* with your actions to produce results. Write your weekly weight loss desire. Example: "Lord, this week it is my desire to lose three pounds." Then ask Him how you should cooperate with Him on this.

On the "Action" side of the paper you might write, "Be faithful every day." Well, you can't be faithful without the Lord. You need your Daily Power Time with Him to strengthen your faith. You may want to subtract calories and add some prayer and Bible-reading time.

One woman wrote as a desire, "To spend more time with the Lord." As an action she had to decide just how she was going to do that, and she had to be specific.

The Lord wants us to be specific. Vagueness never brings beautiful, eternal results.

Actions: In order to spend more time with the Lord, I will turn off the TV set in the afternoons. I will get up a half hour earlier in the morning to pray and read the Word. I'll allow myself time every night before going to bed to pray and read the Word.

What would *your* specific actions be?

Diane D. was puzzled with her Desire-Action Sheet. She didn't honestly know what she wanted of herself. She wondered, "What are my desires?" She knew her mother's desires for her, she knew her husband's desires for her, and her children's, but she wasn't sure of her own.

She was flying to Portsmouth, Virginia, for a seminar of Christian workers and she had hoped to fill out her Desire-Action Sheet on the plane. But she couldn't think of desires *she* had. She knew her husband wanted her to lose weight, but she truly didn't know if *she* wanted to.

When she arrived at the seminar, she stood in a crowd of people and a complete stranger turned to her and said, "Excuse me. I hope you don't mind my speaking up like this, but the Lord was just talking to me about you. He told me that you do not know the desires of your own heart."

Diane's mouth dropped.

"But do you know what else the Lord is showing me?" he continued. "The Lord is showing me that He knows those deep hidden desires you have. It is His great pleasure to reveal to you those deep desires and He wants to fulfill them for you one by one. He needs your attention to show you, though."

It was an experience that was to change Diane's life. She realized she had been afraid to think thoughts for herself or to be in charge of her own life. She began to pray boldly, seeking the Lord for herself and her own walk with the Lord. It wasn't too many days later when she was filling in the Desire side of her sheet. And little by little, one by one, she saw these fulfilled.

Saying One Thing—Doing Another

One good result the Desire-Action Sheet has is revealing the inconsistencies in our words. Often we talk about obeying but we blatantly disobey. We'll pray, "Oh, Lord, I just want to be your obedient servant. I want to delight in you with my heart and soul," and then we'll run to the refrigerator for some high-calorie "treat."

The Lord doesn't reward us with ugly high-calorie "treats." He rewards us with power and strength in the Holy Ghost.

Double-bind type communication is saying one thing, meaning another. I push you away, but I'm saying, "Please love me." I say, "I want to obey you, Lord," on one side of my Desire-Action Sheet, and then I go over my calorie allowance by eating a plateful of crackers and cream cheese.

You may discover you are a lot more rebellious than you ever dreamed. Thank God, He can change all that and save you from the bondage of rebellion. He is Savior. He saves us from ourselves.

We are learning to say one thing and, at last, do the same.

Prayer

Lord, I'm not going to just say you're Lord of my life. I'm going to behave and *act* like you're Lord of my life. I'm going to declare you as Lord in all my actions.

I give you the right to tell me when to get up in the morning, when to go to bed at night, what to eat and what not to eat. I delight in you and I am going to act like it. In Jesus' name, Amen.

ten

Who's Rebellious? Not Me!
(I'll fight to prove it!)

Sandy insisted that she was large-framed and that's why she weighed so much. Her roommates in college agreed with her. (It was easier than arguing.) The truth was, Sandy had 238 pounds on her medium-sized frame. She was plainly obese.

"For He Himself [the Lord] knows our frame" reads Psalm 103:14. We may tell ourselves we're not fat, we're only large-boned, but the Lord knows our frame. We may write our weight on I.D. papers 10 or 15 pounds less than the truth, but the Lord knows our frame.

Minneapolis actor and college instructor, Richard Weed, was doing grade reports one day when a student approached him and asked to see his grade on an exam.

"What? You mean I only got a C on that exam?"

"Yes. That's what you earned. What would you rather have gotten as a grade? An A? A B?"

"Well, I don't know—"

Richard handed him his pen. "Why don't you put the grade you want in the book. Here, go ahead. Do you want an A?"

The boy was speechless.

Then the wise teacher said, "I'll do it for you. I'll erase the C and write an A in its place."

When he finished he looked long at the surprised student. "Tell me," he said, "do you know the material any better now?"

We are what we are no matter what lies we may tell ourselves. We may want to give ourselves A's when we earned C's, and conversely, we may downgrade ourselves. (That's equally deceitful.)

Lack of honesty is a symptom of rebellion. If you can be dishonest in a small thing, you can eventually be dishonest in something big. That something big is your honesty with the Lord. You promise to stick to a certain number of calories but you rebel and binge. Or you promise the Lord to live for Him and His ways, and you rebel and go your own fleshly ways. The Lord wants to save us from the deceitfulness of fleshly ways and give us beautiful, wholesome and complete lives in Him.

Read Isaiah 30:1:

Woe to the rebellious children, declares the Lord.
Who execute a plan, but not Mine,
And make an alliance, but not of My Spirit,
In order to add sin to sin.

What is your most difficult problem with rebellion concerning food? Look at the following check list. Do any of these rebellious statements fit you?

___ I eat without thinking about what I'm eating or how it may defile my body. After I've eaten I feel repentant and remorseful.

___ I don't have anything else going for me in my life except eating. I don't want to give that up, too.

___ I want my_____ (fill in blank). It's not fair that I can't eat_____ (fill in blank) when I want to.

___ It's not my fault that I have a weight problem. It's my mother's fault. She's the one who got me fat in the first place. Now I can't help myself.

___ God knows the pressure and problems I've got in my life and that I eat because of them. Why doesn't God remove them if He wants me to be thin?

___ I asked God to take away my appetite and He didn't do it. He must want me fat.

___ If my husband didn't like to eat a lot of fattening foods, I wouldn't be fat.

___ If my wife didn't cook such fattening foods, I wouldn't be fat.

___ I came from a family of overweight people. That's why I'm overweight.

Add your own statements to the list. You see how dishonest rebellion is? The truth is, nobody else is the cause for your overweight. Other people and factors may be the stimuli that triggers your overeating response, but the only one responsible for your overweight is you.

God wants to take the rebelliousness out of us. He wants to free us from that bondage which is worse than being in any prison. *Whom the Son sets free is free indeed!*

God waits for you to be willing to give up rebellious thoughts and actions.

Therefore the Lord longs to be gracious to you,
And therefore He waits on high to have compassion on you.
For the Lord is a God of justice;
How blessed are all those who long for Him.—Isaiah 30:18

Not long ago the OV office received a letter from a man who lost 84 pounds in prison. Neva Coyle sent a copy of the letter to all the group leaders. The man had read about OV in the newspaper and wrote that he had been in prison 14 years and was more than 80 pounds overweight. Have you ever complained that you couldn't change your eating habits because "the conditions weren't right"?

Did you ever tell the Lord you couldn't possibly lose weight when you have a wedding, a luncheon, a party or Christmas just around the corner? The *conditions* aren't right.

This man found Jesus in prison. Eating prison food, unable to choose his own menus, he went from 249 pounds to 165. He said, in his words, "I made up my mind not to defile a temple of the Holy Spirit."

If you don't think you can possibly lose weight in your present situation, you are mistaken. You CAN do it. God will show you how if you will let Him. Take time to listen to Him speak to you. He speaks to you through His Word and in that still small voice within you.

He, your Teacher, will no longer hide Himself, but your eyes will behold your Teacher. And your ears will hear a word behind you, "This is the way, walk in it," whenever you turn to the right or to the left.—Isaiah 30:20-21

Every speck of rebellion has to leave you. Don't be afraid of the removal process. It's for your beautiful good.

There are two things we can help the Lord with as He removes our rebellion. First,

Be willing to admit we are rebellious.

If you don't think there's a shred of rebellion in you, then you won't know what's happening to you as the Lord tries to remove it. You'll get angry at Him, at yourself and at anyone else around for getting in the way of *your* wants and demands.

Some people do not want to admit they are rebellious, especially overweight people. A woman overweight by at least 50 pounds says defensively, "I like to eat! God knows I like to eat. He made me this way, after all. If He wanted me thin, He should have made me a person without an appetite." In effect, the woman was blaming God. And if she could blame God for her own overeating, she could blame Him for any number of other things in her life. She could blame Him for getting sick, for running out of gas on the highway, for her son's lost mittens, for her husband's lack of enthusiasm for the Gospel, for her daughter's broken marriage, for the death of a parent . . .

She could blame God for everything that ever went wrong in her life.

You must understand that putting blame on God for such things is not the Gospel. It is anti-God. The Bible overflows with instructions to love Him through thick and thin, to praise Him, worship Him, rejoice in Him, love His Word and His promises, be comforted in Him, rest in Him, believe in Him, trust Him.

It is not only ridiculous to blame God for your calamities and sorrows (including weight); it is anti-Gospel. Many of the events in our lives we call tragedies are not tragedies at all. They are really God showing His finest for us by giving us a portion of His love far surpassing anything that went before.

"I'm *not* rebellious. God *knows* how I've suffered in my life. In spite of all I've been through, I'm *still* a Christian, after all." These words come from the mouth of a rebellious person.

"I'm not rebellious" are usually the words of a rebellious person.

When God removes rebellion, the process sometimes stings a little. You want your own way and He wants His. He wants to win over your selfish ways in order that you be the winner.

He understands how we hate to let go of our stubbornness. That's why the Holy Spirit inspired these words in Proverbs 3:11 and 12, which He again repeated in the New Testament in the twelfth chapter of Hebrews:

> *Despise not the chastening of the Lord: neither be weary of His correction; for whom the Lord loveth He correcteth; even as a*

father the son in whom he delighteth. (KJV)

We delight Him, therefore He corrects us!

If your own father didn't delight in you, you now have a Heavenly Father who does. It's a wonderful truth to think about and, if you will think about it with your whole mind, you will find it much easier to give up rebellious eating habits.

For whom the Lord loveth He chasteneth, and scourgeth every son whom He receiveth.—Hebrews 12:6 (KJV)

God disciplines us for our own benefit. He chastens *"for our profit, that we might be partakers of His holiness."*

It may not be fun at first because you may really *want* to eat something fattening and sugar-laden. You may really feel you *deserve* another helping of some rich calorie-coated food. You may be *compelled* to devour something that will only add pounds to you. You may be *driven* to the refrigerator or the cupboards.

The Lord understands these compulsions, drives and neurotic substitutions for *true* comfort and love. But He wants them to leave.

He wants the rebellion removed. He can do a perfect work *if* you will begin by admitting the rebellion in your heart and life.

The second requirement needed to help the Lord remove rebellion in our lives is to *allow Him* to do it!

Allow Him the right to remove the rebellion.

Now no chastening for the present seemeth to be joyous, but grievous.—Hebrews 12:11a (KJV)

"Boy, you can say that again," you say. "You should see how my friends eat! I'm feeling bad enough as it is and then, on top of it, I have to sit and watch them eat the foods I can't have."

. . . nevertheless afterward it yieldeth the peaceable fruit of righteousness unto them which are exercised thereby.—Hebrews 12:11b (KJV)

"But sometimes it's so hard! I get nervous, upset or just plain tired—and I want to eat! I just can't help myself! Sometimes I just don't think I can make it!'"

. . . lift up the hands which hang down and the feeble knees; and make straight paths for your feet, lest that which is lame be turned out of the way; but let it rather be healed.—Verses 12-13 (KJV)

"Healed? Lame? I never thought of rebellion making me lame! Being lame of body would be better than being lame of mind, I'm sure. Oh, I need help!"

This dialogue reflects the hearts of many men and women who have successfully allowed the Lord to go to work on attitudes and ideas.

One woman, 35 pounds overweight, wrote on her OV introductory response sheet, "This is the biggest thing that has ever happened to me. I never saw before how rebellious I have been all these years. I've been angry at life, God and myself, and haven't even known it."

Another woman wrote, "Four years ago I came back to the Lord and He has been everything to me. I thought I had given Him all of my old habits. One habit I didn't give Him was eating.

"I've been on a lot of diets, and each one of them out of pride. I'm beginning to realize how many things I've done out of pride. It's hard to admit, but I believe it was pride that destroyed my marriage. I drove my husband away and now he'll never return."

Many painful and even tragic events take place because of rebellion.

Pride is a form of rebellion because pride resists God's authority and control of your life. Pride is having an inordinate opinion of your own importance, superiority or merit. God wants to free us of these.

He will do it His way and one way to help Him is to rejoice in what He is doing in your life.

Rejoice Evermore

Start attacking rebellion by rejoicing in what God is doing for you. Rejoice in your calorie allowance. Praise the Lord for the number of calories He has given you to eat each day! Thank Him for your new eating program. Thank Him for the new life ahead of you as a thinner person.

There is much for you to rejoice in. He is removing rebellion from you. You will rejoice doubly as you experience the rebellion leaving you.

Prayer

Jesus is Lord! *Peggy Trent* (your name), you are not Lord. *Peggy Trent* (your name), you are controlled by the Holy Spirit. I refuse rebellion. I renounce the hold that rebellion has had over me. Jesus, I put you back on the throne of my life. I will not serve under the rule and weight of my own flesh. I choose reward, not punishment.

Lord, I admit to rebellion in my life.

I <u>willingly</u> turn from these ways and <u>willingly</u> give you the right to change me.

Even though I have been an overeater for *20* (fill in) years, I can be free! Your Word tells me that I do not need to continue as a victim of overeating anymore! <u>I am a new person in Christ</u>!

I will not make excuses for fleshly indulgences.

I will not demand my own way.

I will not hurt my body and mind with rich fattening foods (thinking I'm "pampering" myself).

I will not blame others for what I've done to myself.

I will submit to your discipline.

I will obey you.

I will deny my flesh (by denying myself, I'm really gaining great rewards).

I will rejoice that you are my teacher and you are telling me the way I must walk.

I will rejoice evermore. Thank you, Jesus!

eleven

Why Are We Attracted to the Wrong Foods?

Have you ever noticed that when you overeat, you don't do it with something like carrots or watercress? When is the last time you *craved* a celery stick?

Did you ever binge on lettuce?

Your fleshly indulgences are usually something fattening, most likely something sweet, like dessert.

Whenever Barbara D. had a problem as a teenager, her mother would sit down at the kitchen table with her, bring out the chocolate cake or the blueberry pie and they'd talk over Barbara's problem while eating these and other high-calorie nonspiritual comforters.

Bev. R. remembers when she was sad or upset as a young girl, her mother offered sweets to help her "feel a little better." If she came home from school upset about something a friend had said or done, her mother sliced her a chunk of something fattening, poured her a glass of milk, and said, "You'll feel better after you eat this."

Others share how, as children, they cleaned their plates in order to "earn" dessert. Dessert, for them, became far more important than the meal. Later, when they really wanted to treat themselves, they chose dessert. And they're still choosing dessert.

Are you a chubby member of past Clean Plate Clubs who gobbled up all the food on your plate, even though you were already stuffed to the chin? You did it for the sake of the glimmering-in-the-distance, on the kitchen counter or in the refrigerator, luscious and tantalizing—*dessert*. You even gulped in dreaded sweet potatoes or wrinkled peas and onions—for the glorious reward of *dessert*.

Was that you wiping up every lick of gravy on your plate, choking on those last forkfuls of fried liver because over there just beyond your reach was—oh, too glorious for words—*dessert*!

Nothing was too dear a price to pay for strawberry shortcake or chocolate chiffon pie, or a similar mess. In fact, even fruit cocktail out of the can was worth finishing your artichoke salad.

Did you, at the age of ten, completely wipe out the hunger problem of India by eating every morsel of food on your own plate? Certainly you did. You deserved a reward for that, you say. Your reward was dessert.

For all your consideration toward the millions of starving people of the world, you were rewarded with a fat body and fatter habits. And India is still starving.

Then later, was that you in line at the school cafeteria, passing right by the beautiful vegetables, salads and entrees, heading directly for the desserts?

And how about recently? Wasn't that you, when you were feeling a little blue, comforting yourself with a rich and calorie-loaded *dessert*?

The unconscious desire is to reward suffering. Desserts can become that reward.

Desserts can come in many forms. From pastries to finger sandwiches; from dried fruit to homemade fudge. As long as it's something you like.

If you are a normally healthy (not diabetic or hypoglycemic) and you crave sweets, it may not be sweets you crave at all. Maybe it's energy you need. Sugar raises the blood sugar level in the body and some people get an energy boost after eating it. It's temporary, of course, and after the boost drops, you feel worse than before. So you eat more sugar.

Some Christians walk around droopy, tired and exhausted all the time. If you ask them, "What's new?" they sigh and shrug their shoulders and tell you how tired they are. Worn out. Done in. Pooped. Beat.

Sometimes the reason we're feeling all the above is because we are taking into our own hands what the Lord wants to do. We get worn out in the flesh because we're behaving in the flesh.

There are times we get tired because our bodies are made of flesh, and when they are worked too hard or don't get enough rest, they get tired. It is okay to be tired *some* time. A football player may be tired after practice; a flight attendant may be tired after a long run across the country and back; a teacher may be tired after an evening of correcting papers. These examples are not due to anxiety-tiredness.

Things that make you feel tired:
Allowing yourself to be worried.
Allowing yourself to feel nervous.
Allowing yourself to feel frightened.
Allowing yourself to feel anxious.

The Holy Spirit doesn't drive you, push you, force you or overwork you. He doesn't give you so much work that you can hardly finish it without falling to pieces. Let go of your drives and let Him work through you, accomplishing what *He* desires.

If you're craving an energy boost, your true source of power and strength is waiting for you. The Word of God "rejoices the heart." Absorb and apply the truths and power in the Word to your life. Allow it's energy to permeate your being and see how unappealing a piece of candy or a sweet will seem to you.

When you are not in the Word, you're not receiving your power pack of strength and vitality. Your spirit and soul are not fed on the true source of energy. Caffeine or sugar may be what you think you crave, but actually you need *more*! You need the power of God!

"A joyful heart makes a cheerful countenance," reads the Proverbs. At the same time, a bad mood makes you tired.

Have you ever noticed how tiring it is to be angry or to think a lot of negative thoughts? That is because you were not created to think a lot of negative thoughts. You were created to meditate on the Word of God and communicate with God himself.

As it is written in the book of Joshua, make your prayer: "This book of the law shall not depart out of *my* mouth, but I shall meditate therein day and night, that *I* may observe to do according to all that is written therein; for then *I* will make my way prosperous, and then *I* shall have good success."

One well-known preacher, an ex-fat person, used to be able to eat two and three pies in one sitting. He was so fat he could hardly tie his shoes. He said he wouldn't have dreamed of stuffing himself with asparagus or cauliflower. That would be *punishment*.

What does reward and punishment mean to you? When you

were a child, what were your favorite rewards? Were you rewarded with a "treat" of candy, cookies, ice cream? Do you do the
same thing to your own children? When you give a child a treat,
is it usually a sugar treat?

Punishment

What does punishment mean to you? Doesn't it mean being
deprived of something? When you eat fattening foods, sugar
"treats," rich desserts, you are depriving yourself of a beautiful
body and a healthy mind.

The definition of *punishment* is: a penalty inflicted for an of-
fense or fault. You may think you are rewarding yourself by eating wrong foods, but you are really punishing yourself. You may
joke about healthy low-calorie foods as "punishment," but you
have it confused. There's nothing at all punishing about proper
eating.

The Word of God gives you wisdom regarding the way you
eat. The Word of God makes you smart, not dumb. You are no
longer vain in your imaginings. Your heart is not foolish, nor is it
darkened. You're on the road to wisdom and beauty. You no
longer profess yourself to be wise while actively showing yourself
to be a fool (Rom. 2:21b, 22). You know the difference between
punishment and reward.

In your journal, make a list of good things you'd like to give
yourself. Maybe it's a long, leisurely bubble bath, a long distance
telephone call to a friend, curling up in your favorite chair and
reading a great book (with your extra time gained from less time
spent eating). Maybe it's buying something or going somewhere.
Maybe it's taking time off from a heavy schedule to do nothing at
all, or work on a favorite hobby. On your list, write no foods.

Food is not a friend. Be aware that the advertisements for
food are for one purpose and one purpose
only—to get your money. If you spend
more time eating and preparing food
than you do with Jesus, you have chosen
the wrong friend. If you eat wherever you

go and whenever you sit down, you've got the wrong companion. Jesus is your only true and faithful friend who loves you with the heart of eternity.

Food does not love you.

Love and food have nothing to do with one another. In spite of the fact that our celebrations and festive events are always accompanied by food and feasting, the food itself is not love. It is the *people* who represent the love. If you love food because it makes you feel loved just like when you were a small child when your mama used to feed you, it's your mama you ought to love and remember, not food! Your heart and mind ought to be fixed on loving and caring about *people*.

Food does not make you happy.

God is your happiness. Food is something to eat with care and dedication to the Lord in order to keep your body, which He has given you to care for, *healthy*.

You use food, it doesn't use you.

You say to a pastry, "I don't want to put you into my body even though you'll taste good going down. You aren't of any use to this body. I don't want you." But you say to a ripe juicy apple, "You would be useful to this body. You will also taste delicious. I want you."

One OV member returned from a church supper glowing with delight. The other members of her group were eager to learn how she handled herself at the affair.

"You should have seen all the food they spread out on the tables," she said.

They nodded as people do while listening to unpleasant news.

"Everything was fattening. I mean, everything. As I passed along the length of the table I knew that dish after dish held nothing I could eat. I was really hungry, too. I could have eaten a few of those fattening fruit salad dishes with the whipped cream and marshmallows and told myself, 'Well, what else can I do? I have to eat *something.*' "

If this hasn't happened to you yet, it will some time in the future. You will find yourself in circumstances that make it inconvenient to remain on your new eating program. This woman handled it beautifully.

"I just said to all that food, 'I don't want you. I won't eat you. You are fattening and have no nutritive value. I want to put food into this body that will make it run better.' "

The others understood why she was glowing.

"So I had the most beautiful pile of raw vegetables without dressing. And I ate a bran muffin with it. Total calories: 150."

You don't have to be a victim of circumstances. If there's nothing but fattening food in front of you, change the circumstances. Nobody forces you to eat fattening food. If you eat it, you do it of your own choosing. You don't have to worry about insulting anybody. You don't have to worry about going hungry. You don't have to worry about being different.

Reward!

New ways to reward yourself:

You can change your thinking about rewards. A reward should be something to *benefit* you. Next time for dessert, give yourself something that's *good* for you!

Picture this: You're sitting in a restaurant with somebody you really like and admire. Your friend looks at the menu and orders something greasy, fattening and with only a trace of vitamins or minerals, if any. You're stunned. (You always thought your friend was smart!) Then *you* look at the menu and order broiled fish with no butter and a large salad with fresh lemon juice as dressing. You've just given yourself a fabulous reward. A *reward* is something given or received in return or recompense for service, merit, hardship, etc. You actually pay yourself for staying on your eating program and acting wisely.

You're out with thin friends who are eating fattening, ugly foods, and you have a choice between a green salad and a rich dessert. You choose the salad and thereby reward yourself. "Wise choice," you smile to yourself as you chew a piece of lettuce. "I'm rewarded with good things and a thinner body."

You would have *punished* yourself by eating the rich dessert. You don't deserve to be punished. You deserve to be rewarded with good things, the good things that will make a happier and more beautiful you.

Listening to the Lord and obeying His voice is rewarding yourself. When you hear Him tell you, "Don't eat that," and you obey, you can sing His praises and feel wonderful. When you hear Him tell you, "It's okay to eat that," and you obey His directions, you receive a reward. Your reward is feeling good, blessed, happy, content, pleased. You are making Jesus Lord of your life. Jesus is now on the throne as ruler of your life, not you.

Prayer

Dear Father, in the name of Jesus, I renounce the hold that sweets (name them) have had over me. I refuse an addiction and attraction to sweets. I am not a lover of desserts. I am free by the power of the Holy Spirit within me.

Jesus died on the cross for me to set me free from the addiction to wrong foods. I refuse an attraction and interest in these foods in the name of Jesus.

Father, give me wisdom to understand the difference between reward and punishment. Help me to choose to reward my body, not punish it.

I do not blame my childhood or any person for my overweight. I realize that nobody forces the fork into my mouth. I do it myself. Therefore I break the hold that past habits and experiences have had on me, tempting me to overeat and to eat sweets. Sweets are now ugly to me. I am free from them. They have made my body ugly and I refuse to give them that power over me any longer.

In Jesus' name, Amen.

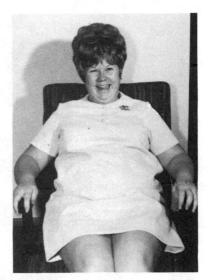

Neva Coyle, founder and director of OV, at 248 pounds, and at the right, 235 (pregnant).

Today Neva weighs 145 pounds.

Carol Ewing before . . .

and after Overeaters Victorious.

This is Diane before the weight-loss program, at 142 pounds.

Diane Brooks at 123 pounds.

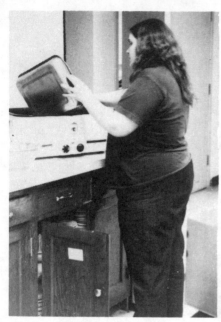

Mary Jo Koplos weighed 250 pounds in this picture.

Her goal weight is 130 pounds. She is well on her way here, at 189.

Look what a weight loss of 47 pounds can do! Cindy Phillips weighed 208 in this photo.

Here she is at 161 pounds. Her goal is 145.

Salli Chaffee, at just 4 feet 11 inches tall, weighed 138 pounds.

She's slimmed down to 110 and 3/4 pounds.

Bonnie Newberg went from 150 pounds . . .

to a lovely 133.

Joyce Svetin (left) weighed 159 pounds in this picture.

Thanks to Overeaters Victorious, she's lost 6 pounds here, and on her way to her goal of 125.

Linda Clark's weight before OV was approximately 145 pounds.

Presently, she weighs 118.

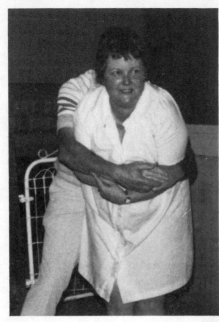

Gloria Wiebusch has lost 80
pounds in the OV program.
Here she is at 190 pounds.

Now she weighs a flattering 131.

Esme Kepple at 168 pounds.

His new creation at 130.

RoseMaree Miller weighed 244 pounds in this picture.

Here she is at 187 and losing in OV.

Nancy Shea started out at 186 pounds . . .

on her journey to her new look, at 127.

Helen Hassler (left) began at 190 pounds.

What a difference 36 pounds can make! Helen at 154.

Joan Webster, 191

Dee Wilcox, 170

Left to right: Joan Webster, 156; Gloria Wiebusch, 132;
Dee Wilcox, 148; Kay Lineer, 129.

Gloria Wiebusch, 211

Kay Lineer, 143 1/2

Sharing victories

Over a thousand pounds lost to the glory of God! We'll never weigh the same again.

Marie Chapian, author, with the OV group of women who cooperated so enthusiastically so that the message could be shared with others.

twelve

Knowing the Will of the Lord

> *My son [or My daughter], give attention to my words; Incline your ear to my sayings. Do not let them depart from your sight; Keep them in the midst of your heart. For they are life to those who find them, and health to all their whole body.*—Proverbs 4:20-22

Did you know that obesity is not healthy? How many times have you visited someone with a highly contagious disease, such as hepatitis or mononucleosis, and thrown your arms around them, hugging and kissing them? How many times have you asked to borrow the toothbrush of someone with the flu?

Those examples might sound unlikely, but millions of people every day harm their bodies in foolish ways. Think of the ways you have made your body fat and unhealthy. Consider the heaps of french fries you've consumed in your lifetime, the pounds of chocolate, the rivers of ice cream. The average American eats 95 pounds of sugar a year, almost 8 pounds every month. Our teeth, bones, liver, heart, skin and nerves show the damage.

The Word of God leads us into health. The Word of God *is* our health. If you love God, your love for your own body (the temple dwelt in by the Holy Spirit) will motivate you to take excellent top-notch care of it.

> *Put away from you a deceitful mouth, and put devious lips far from you.*—Proverbs 4:24

The Word of God does away with "devious lips"; in our case, it's devious *eating* lips.

The will of the Lord is that we live in honesty and truth. Our actions and deeds should not be hidden behind the pantry door. The will of the Lord is that our lives be pure enough not to shame us at any time.

You can shout praises to the Lord, and sing, "Hallelujah, Jesus is Lord of my life," and then minutes later steal away to the refrigerator where you slurp in half a can of Reddi-Whip squirted on your finger!

One woman shared how she sang, "Take my life and let it be, consecrated Lord to thee . . ." in the morning church service, but that night lay on her bed sick from stuffing herself with food all day.

It is not God's will that we kill ourselves with a fork and spoon. We were born to eat, not to diet or binge. It is God's will that our enemy, "Lack of Discipline," be destroyed in us.

It is not God's will that we be addicted to junk food and sweets. Some people take Kool-Aid, soda and other sugar drinks like a fix. They have their regular fix of cookies and cupcakes, not unlike the dope addict who is hooked on drugs. One of the differences is, the food junkie has a readier and cheaper supply at hand.

Eating the foods that Jesus would eat takes a little thought. Remember, we can be victims of *advertising.* Our source of nutritional knowledge shouldn't come from the magazines, TV and radio ads. If the wrapper on the bread says, "Eat this; it's good for you," don't buy it without reading what's in it. *You* decide if it's nutritious enough to eat.

Your Will and God's!

"I've been dishonest with myself and God for years," one woman shared. "I know what it's like to *not* want to eat something and then eat it. I've even eaten things like the burnt cookies out of the batch I'm baking just because I didn't want to throw them away. I mean, they taste awful. Yet I've eaten them."

Devious lips gulp in burnt cookies as if they didn't have calories. Devious lips also lick the finger after running it over the edge of the children's sandwiches. Devious lips eat up the last of the food in the serving dishes while clearing the table. Devious lips scrape up the cake crumbs from around the cake and gobble them up.

Three or four burnt cookies, a dollop of peanut butter and jelly and a handful of cake crumbs could add over 500 calories to your daily allowance. If you are on a 1,000 calorie a day diet, you just ate up one-half of your day's food and you may not have even counted it.

A deceitful mouth is a grumbling mouth. Deceit is lying. *The devil is a liar and the father of lies* (John 8:44). When you grumble, you are lying. You are saying things like, "He gets to order a rich dessert and I have to eat cottage cheese. Who needs all this suffering? This is awful!"

The *truth* is, "Praise God, I'm eating beautiful cottage cheese and he's eating that ugly dessert. Thank God I do not have to eat the way he does. I can refrain. I can say no. Thank God for the power of the Holy Spirit dwelling in me. Thank you, Jesus, for strength and help."

Remember your grateful heart will wash away the deceit of the enemy's lies. Your grateful heart won't allow your mouth to spew deceit. You won't lie, complain or grumble. Your grateful heart swells with love and gratitude, and even if you stumble, you can say, "I'm sorry," and pick yourself up again and start anew.

You say happily, "Lord, I love you enough to eat 1,000 (or whatever) calories a day!" Don't plan any failures. You cannot lose with Jesus.

It is the will of the Lord that we not be defiled by the ways of the world. It is God's will that we

> . . . *be filled with the knowledge of His will in all spiritual wisdom and understanding, so that you may walk in a manner worthy of the Lord, to please Him in all respects, bearing fruit in every good work and increasing in the knowledge of God; strengthened with all power, according to His glorious might, for the attaining of all steadfastness and patience; joyously.*—Colossians 1:9b-11

Meditate on the above verses. Write them in your journal. Repeat them over and over. Think about them. Paraphrase them. Think about them some more. Those words hold such magnificent promises and claims for us, we could spend a lifetime searching out their meaning and applying it to our lives.

"Attaining steadfastness and patience *joyously*"—what words! This tells us that losing weight can be a joyous thing. We're attaining steadfastness by sticking to a calorie allowance and patience by seeing the pounds fall off far more slowly than we'd like them to. It's joyous!

When you are considering God's will for you, think about His *daily* will for you. What is His will for me *today*? Then, according to the above verse, as you are filled with the knowledge of His will in all spiritual wisdom and understanding, you know why obeying His will is important.

In your journal, on a separate page, draw a line down the center of the paper. On one side, write, GOD'S WILL FOR ME TODAY IS THAT I: On the other side, write the spiritual wisdom and understanding you'll be gaining with the word WHY?

Here is an example:

God's-Will-for-Me-Today Chart

God's will for me today is that I:	Why?
1. Stay faithful to my calorie allowance.	To stay in close communication with Him, so close that I lose the compulsion to overeat.
2. Fill in my calorie log daily.	
3. Be responsible for what I eat.	
4. Start today to take off the last 20 pounds to reach my goal weight.	To glorify Him and be a beautiful witness of His power in my life.
5. Have a long Daily Power Time with Him and skip TV.	When I miss my Daily Power Time or take just a quickie, I don't soak in enough strength to overcome the temptation to overeat. (When I'm out of the Word, I eat more.)
6. Do something creative that I enjoy (sewing, carpentry, pottery, painting, etc.).	To give me fun and relaxation, something I enjoy to do, and a sense of accomplishment. (I tend to eat when I feel bored or useless.)
7. Finish a task or assignment that I've put off.	To remove frustration from me. (I eat when I'm frustrated, and unfinished work that piles up frustrates me.)

We know God's will by knowing His Word. The more you meditate in the Word, the more of Him, His mind, His purposes,

His wisdom, His understanding, and His eternal purpose for your life you gain.

You can't obey His will unless you *know* His will. Jesus said, "For whoever does the will of My Father who is in heaven, he is My brother and sister and mother" (Matt. 12:50), showing us how close we can be to Him *if* we know His will!

We learn His will from His Word. In the Word you learn how Jesus acted, spoke, prayed, thought. He is our model. He said, "And He who sent Me is with Me; He has not left Me alone, for I always do the things that are pleasing to him" (John 8:29). It is His will that we be pleasing to Him.

It is God's will that you gain wisdom and understanding in caring for your own body and the bodies of your loved ones.

World Food vs. Kingdom Food

The foods that have defiled our bodies are foods that have appealed to our flesh, not our spirit. The Bible tells us that we are living in a world dominated by sin, but we are born-again creatures, "not of this world," and, not to be *dominated* by the world and its ways.

Jesus prayed to His Father in John 17, "I have given them [you and me] Thy word; and the WORLD has hated them, because they are not of the world, even as I am not of the world" (v. 14).

Do you think that bag of tootsie rolls in the candy store has your name on it? Are the smells coming from that pizza parlor calling you *personally* to their doors?

Jesus prayed to the Father not to remove those beckoning smells and sights from you, but to *keep you from succumbing*.

I do not ask Thee to take them out of the world, but to keep them from the evil one. They are not of the world, even as I am not of the world. —John 17:15, 16

And just when you're ready to plunge headlong into the Halloween glop in your child's trick or treat bag, *a ploy of the world direct from "Destruction Headquarters,"* you hear, "You needn't fall prey to that. Depend on Me. I've overcome the world. I've overcome holiday eats and candies."

Alice R. used to bake cookies for the family and then eat them all herself before the children arrived home from school. When the children walked in the door, they smelled the aroma of the baked cookies, but found no cookies. Alice had to quickly whip up some extra batches in order not to face the disgrace of what she had done.

God so loved the *world* (you and me who live in the world and are living in the midst of its ways and influences) that He sent His only Son, Jesus, to die on the cross for us and by believing in Him, have eternal life and power and strength to live each day above the cares of this world.

The world offers a lot of terrible stuff to put into your body. It even offers supposedly low-calorie products that are just as harmful to your body as sugars, starches and processed foods. Artificial sweeteners, chemicals, additives, preservatives, etc., have long been the outrage of nutritionists who publish lengthy tomes on their dangers to the human body.

We suggest that if you're accustomed to putting sugar in your hot drink, please don't switch to saccharin or a chemical sugar substitute. Try to eat more natural sugar from fresh fruit. Try cooking with honey, maple syrup, sorghum, blackstrap molasses (Count the calories, though! One tablespoon honey equals 65 calories) and fresh fruit juices.

Be of good cheer. Chin up. Feel good. Rejoice! Jesus has overcome the world. He has overcome sugar, sweets, starches, chemical sweeteners—the ugly gooey stuff meant to load your veins with cholesterol and crowd your organs with fat and disease.

For all that is in the world, the lust of the flesh and the lust of the eyes and the boastful pride of life, is not from the Father, but is from the world. And the world is passing away, and also its lusts; but the one who does the will of God abides forever.—1 John 2:16, 17

Maybe at one time you loved the junk food and sweets and you were fat because of it, but now you are free to love healthy Kingdom food and be thin because of it.

Do not love the world, nor the things in the world. If anyone loves the world, the love of the Father is not in him.—1 John 2:15

You are a child of God. You are now free to eat foods that feed your body and make it strong. The whole world lies in the power of the evil one, but you are no longer a victim of the world and its fattening foods.

Kingdom Food

Protein foods: Fish (not the breaded kind fried in grease), fresh or frozen, broiled or baked, or steamed

Canned water-packed tuna, salmon, sardines

Chicken (without the skin) or turkey, broiled, baked or steamed

Fresh eggs poached, boiled, fried in nonstick pans, scrambled with cheese

Cottage cheese (lo-cal)

Cheeses (not processed American)

Lean meats

Whole-grain breads, muffins, rolls and cereals (a huge variety to choose from)

Wheat germ, bran

Vitamin and mineral feasts: Fresh vegetables of all kinds served in dozens of fabulous salad combinations

Homemade dressings prepared with natural ingredients

Cooked or steamed vegetables, eaten hot and crisp without butter (or very little)

Beautiful fresh fruit of every kind eaten raw or cooked in a myriad of delightful combinations or eaten singly

Drinks of fresh fruit or vegetable juices without added sugar.

We are no longer ignorant of the harmful effects of sugar and artificial sweeteners on our bodies. This information isn't a secret any more. One man tells how he preached at his children about the dangers of tobacco. "Look at the warning on the wrapper!" he'd tell them. Then he looked at the label of his artificially sweetened so-called "diet soda." There's a warning there, too. He realized his responsibility as a Christian is not only to be informed, but also to respond appropriately to that information.

It's a known fact that overdoses of artificial sweeteners cause cancer in laboratory animals. Extended use in the diets of children could lead to cancer in their adult years. Before you throw your hands in the air and yell, "There's not a thing a person can eat any more! Everything causes cancer!" let's take the matter to the Lord. What do these facts mean to us as Christians and what does the Lord say to us about them?

OV does not tell you to stop eating harmful foods, but we ask you to talk to the Lord about your responsibility in the light of the known facts.

You ought to feel good about yourself. The Lord loves you so wonderfully. "My love and kindness shall not depart from you, nor shall My covenant of peace and completeness be removed, says the Lord, Who has compassion on you" (Isa. 54:10b) Amp. Bible.

Feel good about yourself and don't take the fun out of eating. Enjoy healthy vitamin-rich foods. Let your body, soul and spirit glorify the Lord.

Prayer

Thank you, Jesus, for Kingdom food that makes my body alive with vitality and strength. Thank you, Jesus, for Kingdom food that builds muscles, restores worn tissues, makes bones, teeth, gums, hair and skin healthy and strong.

Thank you, Jesus, for the power to overcome devious lips and a deceitful mouth. Thank you for overcoming the world for me. Thank you, Jesus, for power to overcome the attraction to the world's foods.

Thank you, Jesus, for the power of your Word in my life. Thank you for your promises now coming true in my life. Thank you for your wonderful Word which has become health to my whole body, just as you said it would.

I love you,

_____

Your name

thirteen

Budgeting Calories and Nutrition

Now that you're no longer a chump for wrong foods, you'll want to budget your calories in food groups. Decide how many calories you're going to spend on protein for the day, how many on fruit, grains, vegetables, juices.

It's necessary to know the nutritive content of foods to know the best sources of various nutrients that your body needs. The more varied your diet the better. *All* nutrients are essential for good health and nutrition.

A common error dieters make in meal planning is emphasizing one type of food and excluding others. If you concentrate your eating program on only one or two types of foods, you'll suffer a lack of necessary elements, including *protein, fats, carbohydrates, mineral salts and vitamins*, all vitally necessary for your body to function fabulously.

As tissues are broken down in your body, the wastes are eliminated and the tissues replaced and replenished by the foods you eat. If one essential element is missing from your diet, your health will suffer.

Protein (fish, eggs, chicken, turkey, cheese, cottage cheese, lean meats) supplies muscle-forming elements and acts as fuel for energy. *Carbohydrates* and *fats* (protein foods, whole grain foods, natural sugars) provide heat and energy to the body system and influence protein metabolism. Vitamins and minerals (fruits and vegetables) are crucial in keeping the metabolism in good working order.

Protein

The word *protein* is derived from the Greek word meaning "to take first place." Protein foods are of first importance in the diet. Your body needs the carbohydrate and fat found in protein-rich foods. (This doesn't mean the grease from a fatty steak or hamburger or the melted butter on your popcorn. There is absolutely no protein in butter or grease.)

Some proteins are superior in quality to others. For example, fish, which is close to meat in protein content, has been found to be superior in protein quality.

The Food and Nutrition Board recommends the following protein allowance for adults: 65 grams for the 153-pound man, 55 grams for the 128-pound woman. This figures about .45 grams per pound of body weight. You figure your protein allowance on your *ideal* weight, not what you actually do weigh.

Dr. George Watson, author of "Nutrition and Your Mind," finds that the recommended daily allowance of one gram of protein for each 2.2 pounds of body weight is adequate to meet most needs.[1]

Nutritionists claim protein intake should be higher when losing weight, but not to exceed 100 grams a day.

The best sources of protein are animal sources such as milk, eggs, cheese, meat, poultry and fish for highest biological value. Three of these foods alone can provide 51 grams of protein. They are one pint of milk, one egg and four ounces of meat or meat substitutes (fish, poultry, cheese). Grains such as wheat, soybeans, corn, rice, as well as nuts, peas, beans, lentils and peanuts provide a second source of protein.[2]

Weight-loss diets that advocate eating only protein foods are not wise to follow. They do not only rob your body of the valuable vitamins and minerals it needs to function properly, but nutritionists consider excess protein a health hazard due to the uric acid and toxic substances that produce fermentation in the body. Too much protein results in putrification in the body. Too much carbohydrate produces fermentation. (You can see why God admonishes us to avoid excesses!)

Nutritional Awareness

It is important that you have nutritional awareness. Misinformation abounds left and right. Suppose one day someone tells you banana skins are a miracle food and eating thirty a day will add years to your life. Another day you may hear that if you eat a bushel of watermelon seeds a day, your hair will grow thicker and longer. Or suppose someone tells you sugar won't hurt you; it just flushes right through the body. Or you hear, "You don't need protein three times a day," or "It's okay to skip meals. You lose weight that way," or "Taking vitamin supplements won't help the body at all." All of these are not only humorous, but incorrect.

It's important that *you* know what's going on nutritionally so that *you* develop your own program in wisdom and truth. In order for your body to be healthy and strong, you need to be informed and intelligent about food and its nutrients. Health and your forever-thin body won't happen by accident. You make it happen.

A common malady of fat people is that they do not *want* to know about nutrition because it may mean they'll have to change their buying and eating habits. You are now past that point in your new road to thinness and health. You have already committed yourself to losing weight. Now you are learning how to do it wisely. You are learning how to bless your own body.

You are becoming aware of:

1. How the body functions utilize each food nutrient.
2. What the body requirements are for optimum health and vitality.

Below is a daily food guide published by the U.S. Department of Agriculture. It shows you clearly that each nutrient is important to your health.

A Daily Food Guide*

Milk Group (8-ounce cups)
> 2 to 3 cups for children under nine years
> 3 or more cups for children nine to twelve years
> 4 cups or more for teenagers
> 2 cups or more for adults
> 3 cups or more for pregnant women
> 4 cups or more for nursing mothers

---

*"Consumers All Yearbook of Agriculture, 1965," U.S. Department of Agriculture, Washington, D.C., 1965, p. 394.

Meat Group
Two or more servings. Count as one serving:
    2 to 3 ounces lean, cooked beef, veal, pork, lamb, poultry,
        fish—without bone
    2 eggs
    1 cup cooked dry beans, dry peas, lentils
    4 tablespoons peanut butter

Vegetable/Fruit Group (1/2 cup serving or 1 piece fruit, etc.)
Four or more servings per day, including:
    1 serving of citrus fruit, or other fruit or vegetable as a good
        source of vitamin C, or 2 servings of a fair source
    1 serving, at least every other day, of a dark-green or deep-
        yellow vegetable for vitamin A
    2 or more servings of other vegetables and fruits, including
        potatoes

Breads/Cereals Group
Four or more servings daily (whole-grain, enriched or restored).
Count as one serving:
    1 slice bread
    1 ounce ready-to-eat cereal
    1/2 to 3/4 cup cooked cereal, cornmeal, grits, macaroni, noo-
        dles, rice or spaghetti

Overeaters Victorious recommends a diet guideline adaptable
to any daily calorie limit. You will find it an introduction to a
simple way to eat. It is found at the end of this book. You may
want to use this to guide your daily calorie allowance. It is important to eat a balanced diet each day and important you don't
skip meals.

Why it doesn't help you to skip meals:
Each meal you eat (particularly a high-protein meal) increases metabolism and burns up fat deposits. By eating three
high-protein, low-fat meals, you actually lose weight faster than
if you skipped meals or went on a starvation diet. Protein three
times a day keeps your blood sugar level high and aids in pre-
venting hunger pangs. Your body makes use of the food you eat
in a steady, timed manner when you eat three meals a day. Worn
out tissues are repaired, energy is released and utilized and your
body functions in an orderly way, as God planned it to.

Prayer

Dear Lord, help me to develop an interest in nutrition and what my body needs to function beautifully for your glory. I choose to be wise in my eating habits and I choose your wisdom in the foods I put into my body.

I confess and renounce my old habits of eating too much of one food to the exclusion of another. I confess and renounce skipping meals and then binging at the next one. I confess and renounce being ignorant about nutrition and how to eat. I confess and renounce laziness and irresponsibility in food preparation. I confess and renounce buying foods through lust and greed rather than in wisdom and understanding. I confess and renounce stubbornness and rebellion against your divine plan for my nutrition and health. I confess and renounce the lusts of my flesh and appetite. I renounce the lusts for those foods that are harmful to my body.

I refuse to be a friend of the world's system and foods. I choose to eat Kingdom food to the glory of God. In Jesus' name, Amen!

Submit therefore to God. Resist the devil and he will flee from you.—James 4:7

1. Watson, Dr. George, *Nutrition and Your Mind* (Bantam Books), New York, 1974.

2. Null, Gary and Steve and Staff of Nutrition Institute of America, *Protein for Vegetarians* (Jove Publications), New York, 1978.

fourteen

How to Get Self-control When You Don't Think You Have Any

Carolyn D. was once a heavy smoker and smoked as many as five packages of cigarettes a day. She also drank heavily. When she became a Christian she gave her life to the Lord, allowing Him to work His will in her. The first things she wanted to be free from were smoking and drinking. She mentioned how the Lord marvelously helped her overcome her smoking habit. She prayed and asked Him to deliver her from the cigarettes and He did. She withdrew "cold turkey" from five packs a day to none.

The next thing she wanted to be rid of in her life was the drinking. She knew that if she didn't stop, she could well become an alcoholic. Drinking had become a life-style and she enjoyed it too much to be safely in the limits of moderation.

So she simply stopped. She drinks fruit and vegetable juices now. "I can't say it was really that hard to stop smoking and drinking," she said. "I gave these things up for Jesus and I felt really good about it."

But Carolyn is morose and depressed, and telling herself she is a failure. "I have no self-control. I'm overweight and I just can't seem to stop eating."

You can see how wrong she is. With the Lord's help she has successfully gotten rid of two enormous strongholds in her life. Now she has an opportunity to get rid of a third. But instead of looking at her overweight as an opportunity, she saw it as a curse.

Helen O. had a habit of using foul language that earned her the nickname "Garbage Mouth." She swore and cursed with such a rapid flow of filth that even she would be repulsed. "It was awful. I cursed every time I opened my mouth. I gave my heart to Jesus and at first nothing changed with my mouth. Then gradually, as I asked Him to help me stop swearing, He began to help me. I worked at it and totally stopped. I don't even say 'heck or darn' now. Thank God, I'm free. It was like living in hell and speaking its language."

But Helen O. despairs over her 20 pounds of extra weight on her body. "I just don't seem to have any self-control," she says.

We need to understand three things about self-control. *First*, God is the giver of all gifts and the fruit of the Spirit is accomplished by His presence within you. Fruit is *accomplished*, not given. Self-control is a fruit of the Holy Spirit.

Secondly, when we ask God to do something in our lives, He will do it *with our consent and effort*. (See Your Will and God's, chapter twelve.) If you ask God to get you to church on time, He can't very well do it if you don't get out of bed when He awakens you.

Self-control is saying to yourself, "Self, get out of bed."

Thirdly, self-control is something you exercise every day of your life. *You* are in control of your *self*. In order to read this book, you had to pick it up, you had to turn the pages, you had to put your eyes on the pages and decipher the words. You exercised *control* of your *self* and did these things. Nobody else did them for you. If someone is reading this book to you, it's *your* ears doing the listening. You are in control.

If you think you have no self-control in your life because you're overweight, take a look at some other areas in your life where you do exercise self-control. Do you:

____ Get out of bed when the alarm clock rings?

____ Arrive at work on time?

____ Answer the phone when it rings?

____ Pay a bill?

____ Make a decision about anything?

____ Brush your teeth?

____ Take a bath or shower?

____ Resist the urge to do *one* thing you'd like to do, but know you shouldn't so you don't?

If you can check these YES, then you can see how you do *not* lack self-control in your life at all. You're loaded with it!

List some of the bad habits and fleshly indulgences that you have already given up in your life (i.e., drugs, smoking, drinking, swearing, lying, gossiping, cheating, stealing, biting your nails, bed-wetting, thumb-sucking, scratching, oversleeping, habitual lateness, lustful thoughts, etc.). Take time to think about this list. If you can put *one* thing on your list, you have proven that you *do* have self-control.

Now let's bring this self-control to the surface and let it work for you in the area of your weight.

Overeating belongs in the same camp of indulgences as those on the previous list. When Carolyn G. says, "I have victory in the areas of smoking and drinking, but not in eating," she is not quite accurate. The truth is, she has victory in all three because they are, in fact, one area. If you can quit smoking and drinking, you can quit overeating. Some people continue to overeat because they are really *still* smoking and drinking *through* the overeating.

You *do* have self-control. You're lying to yourself if you say you don't. When you read verses in the Bible that say, *"Watch over your heart with all diligence, for from it flow the springs of life,"* and, *"Let your eyes look directly ahead, and let your gaze be fixed straight in front of you"* (Prov. 4:23, 25), you are reading about self-control. When you make a decision, any decision, you are exercising self-control. When you exert effort to do something that is difficult to do, you are exercising self-control. (See the children's book, *I Learn About the Fruit of the Holy Spirit*, by Marie Chapian.)

What Gives Me Self-control?

Please realize that you do have self-control. You use your self-control every day in some way or another. God brings self-control into your life through a variety of ways. Some of these ways you might not like, but some of them you will. Thank God for the privilege to learn self-control!

Psalm 119:65-68 says:

Thou hast dealt well with Thy servant, O Lord, according to Thy word.

(In His Word is everything we could possibly need in this life to teach us and guide us into every fulfillment and joy. He does deal well with us.)

Teach me good discernment and knowledge, for I believe in Thy commandments.

(Teach me, Lord, why it is I could stop biting my fingernails but I can't stop overeating.)

Before I was afflicted I went astray.

(Before I piled all this fat on my body, I went far away from self-control and godliness and overate.)

But now I keep Thy word.

(Your word to me is that you want me to eat _____ calories a day and lose _____ pounds.)

Thou art good and doest good.

(If anybody blows it, I do. But thank you, Jesus, you forgive me when I blow it.)

Teach me Thy statutes.

(I'm desperate enough and afflicted with enough fat now to want to hear your voice and your will for my body.)

It is good for me that I was afflicted, that I may learn Thy statutes.—Psalm 119:71

(I never dreamed there'd be anything good about being fat, but Lord, it has brought me to this point in my life with you where I am willing to learn your will, your law, your rules. It is good for me that I gained weight so that through my overweight and fat, I can become a far more powerful Christian than I otherwise would have chosen to be.)

One woman paraphrased verse 71 to read, "Because I am fat, I am now learning about self-control. I can arrive at the maturity held out to me from the Lord *faster* than if I were not fat. It is good for me that I have been afflicted with fat in order that I can reach such a wonderful nose-to-nose position with God."

This is a beautiful place to be with the Lord. "*I shall delight in Thy statutes*" (Ps. 119:16a) is your new life-song. You delight with your glass of water when everyone else is eating chocolate pie. You delight in your lean meat, broiled chicken, fish, fresh vegetables and fruits, whole grains and fresh eggs and cheeses. What a *delight* to weigh in each week and see God chiseling the fat off your body.

The way to get self-control when you don't think you have any is:

1. *Realize you do have self-control.* It's simply untrue that you have no self-control. You exercise self-control every day of your life. You are exercising self-control right now by reading this book. You're telling yourself what to do and you are doing it.

2. *Stop being hard on yourself.* God knows your frame. He knows that you are a human being and endowed with human characteristics. "He regards the lowly," it says in Psalm 138:6. "He remembers us in our low estate" (Ps. 136:23). "The Lord preserveth the simple: I was brought low, and He helped me" (Ps. 116:6).

David agonized in plea after plea for the Lord to rescue him from out of his troubles and weaknesses. He knew that he couldn't win any battle or overcome any struggle without the help of the Lord. He knew it because he knew that as a human being, he simply wasn't equipped to do it in his own strength.

The Lord tells us this dramatic truth, that *[His] strength is made perfect in weakness* (2 Cor. 12:9, KJV).

"LET THE WEAK SAY I AM STRONG!" He shouts from heaven (Joel 3:10, KJV).

3. *Rejoice in the self-control you do have.* Pat yourself on the back, celebrate. Every time you move the plate of cookies away from you, give yourself a warm grin, a loving nod of approval. Tell yourself, "Good for me!" Every time you order a salad when everyone else is eating something rich and calorie-laden, celebrate your wise choice by a long and leisurely good thought about yourself. Every time you push yourself away from the table instead of eating dessert, rejoice. Shout a hoot of approval.

When is the last time you said, "Hurrah for me!" or "I did it!" or "Good for me!"? Start saying these things about yourself. You're terrific!

You *do* have self-control!

Prayer

Thank you, dear Jesus, for the self-control that I *do* have. Thank you, dear Jesus, that the self-control in my life is accomplished by your presence within me.

Now, in the name of Jesus, I choose to exercise this fruit of the Holy Spirit in a more dynamic way than ever before in my life. I unleash unused God-given strengths and abilities within me and call upon self-control to show itself prominently in my life.

I choose to exercise self-control in the area of food! I choose to demonstrate self-control over the following: (List those foods which have been your weakness.)

Reeses   _rich creamy desert_

french fries   _eating too many raisen_

fattening sauces   _using too much mayo_

pie, cake + icecream   _or salad dressing._

In Jesus' name, I am victorious over these temptations! Amen.

fifteen

What to Do When You Blow It

What happened? You say you just prayed for self-control and you made a list of binge food you won't ever allow to touch your lips again, and then you—you—oh, no, you ate *what*?

You're feeling miserable, your face is covered with guilt. Your stomach is sick, your head is sick, your toes are sick. You would just like to curl up in a ball and turn into a doorknob.

What's the use? you wonder. All is hopeless. All is defeat and doom. "Oh, God, why was I born?" you ask. If you didn't say it, you're thinking it. What a horrible cross to bear—this overeating thing. Why doesn't God just remove it from me? Where is He when I need Him?

Oh, misery, oh, rottenness!

Now, wait a minute. So you blew it. But it's not the first time, you say. You say you blew it last week, too, and the week before that.

Well, that certainly proves one thing, doesn't it? You are a human being and human beings are, in themselves, weak. It also proves that you have the strength to pick yourself up and start all over again because the Lord tells us, "Let the weak say I am strong."

You can't do that, you say? Feeling too rotten. In fact, you feel so rotten, you'd like to go eat something. That way the guilt you are already feeling would have some more guilt to keep itself company. Then you could be even more miserable than you are right now. The more miserable you feel, the more you eat. The more you eat, the more miserable you feel.

Right from the pit.

Imagine yourself walking by one of your past-favorite bakeries. In days gone by you couldn't resist going in, buying something and eating it. But now since you've begun your new eating program, you haven't gone into that bakery once and you haven't eaten one thing of theirs. You've had wonderful self-control. But today it's past lunch time and you didn't have much breakfast and the smells of the bakery are thick in the air . . .

A tempting voice right outside your ear says to you, "Why not have something from the bakery? It won't hurt you. Go ahead. You can count it as your lunch. Besides, you had such a teensy weensy breakfast. Don't you feel weak? Sure you do. What you need is a little pick-me-up."

You try to protest. "But I made a commitment. I—I—" Now you're passing the door. The little voice at your ear says, "Look at those fresh things in the window. No, don't turn away your head. What harm can a little peek do? Look! Your favorite! Remember in the old days how you could eat _____ of those at a time?"

You turn, you look, you lust. You're salivating now. "That's right," says the little voice; "don't they look *delicious*? Why not go inside? You could buy something to bring home for the family!"

That did it. Of course! You'll do it for others! So you barrel into the store, your eyes ablaze with excitement. You buy an armful of baked goods and stumble out, telling yourself what a nice soul you are to think of others before yourself.

By the next corner you've already eaten two chocolate-covered doughnuts, and by the time you get to the bus stop or to your car, you've polished off half the cookies, too.

The little voice at your ear isn't saying much now, but once in a while between chomps you think you hear unpleasant laughter.

By the time you get home, you've eaten the bread, the cake and the fruit bars. There are only two doughnuts left. How can you bring home only two doughnuts, plain at that. You wouldn't want to do that. There's no alternative but to eat them, too. So before getting out of the car, you wolf in the last two doughnuts.

Now the voice at your ear returns. There it is, loud and clear. You hear it as you stagger like a drunk into your house. "*Now* you did it, fatso!" You belch miserably. "Oh, now I did it," you repeat.

The voice sneers, "You haven't got a shred of self-control in you! You are really a failure! Forget it for you, kiddo! You blew it! What a tub of lard you are! Oh, you'll pay for this binge, all right!"

You are utterly crushed and condemned.

You don't want to talk to anyone or see anyone. You're nauseous and dizzy. You hurt all over. You just want to crash into bed and sleep forever. Or sit down and stare at TV.

Do you see the pattern in all this? The devil, who is the father of lies, speaks untruth always. He is the original liar and he roars around like a lion seeking whom he can devour with those lies of his. He appeals to your flesh, the weak part of you. Then, when you fall prey to his lies, he shrieks with torrents of condemning words. He'll call you names; he'll say how disgusting you are; how unloved, how hopeless, how fat and ugly. He'll tell you nobody loves you, you're miserable and will always be miserable. He's got you where he wants you—right in the position where you'll listen to him and believe every word he tells you.

If Satan can get you to feel wretchedly guilty, he's got you in his clutches. For this reason it's very important that you recognize his tactics. All right, you blew it. So what? Pick yourself up and continue on. Your eating program is not geared to last for just a couple of weeks or months. It is a lifelong commitment. No matter how many times you blow it, you're not going to give up. So you blew it at breakfast. Go back on the program at lunch. Write down in your journal the calories you eat, no matter how many.

Remember, overeating can be one of the traits of rebellion and selfishness. You may not *want* to write down the calorie amount on your binge. Maybe you rebel at the idea. Please go back to chapter ten on rebellion and re-read it. Pray the prayer at the end again. Don't be afraid to start over. It's okay, the Lord is with you and He loves you in spite of everything. With this knowledge, the devil will not be able to continue his disgusting game. He'll see that you're not going to sink into guilt and despair every time you blow it. You're confessing your sins to God and you're refusing to hate yourself. God wants you to love yourself. The devil wants you to hate yourself.

God tells us to love our neighbors as *ourselves*; that means we should have an abundance of healthy sound love for ourselves first. As a result of this love, we love others. God wants you to love yourself, and because you belong to Him, you naturally want what He wants. You belong to God. You are His. You aren't something for the devil to manipulate like a plaything.

The Lord is saying to you:

Do not fear, for I am with you;
Do not anxiously look about you, for I am your God.
I will strengthen you, surely I will help you,
Surely I will uphold you with My righteous right hand. —Isaiah
41:10

He is right there with you. As you confess what you did, asking for His forgiveness, He is right there to forgive you!

He forgives all your sins for the asking. Every calorie that you eat beyond your allowance, every tidbit you sneak, every time you cheat, every lie that you have told yourself and believed, every indulgence, EVERYthing—

He forgives.

If we confess our sins, He is faithful and righteous to forgive us our sins and to cleanse us from all unrighteousness. —1 John 1:9

I, even I, am He that blotteth out thy transgressions for mine own sake, and will not remember thy sins. —Isaiah 43:25 (KJV)

I have wiped out your transgressions like a thick cloud, and your sins like a heavy mist. Return to Me, for I have redeemed you. —Isaiah 44:22

Return unto Him. It's okay, return and go on with the program. If you overate at 10:30 in the morning, don't tell yourself you'll go back on your program tomorrow; do it at lunch! Count your calories and have a good lunch within your calorie limit. Don't skip meals and try to atone for your sins.

When You Eat More Than Your Calorie Allowance, Should You Atone for It and Fast the Next Meal or Meals?

This is a familiar syndrome. Binge/Fast. Binge/Fast. Before long it becomes Binge/Binge.

You think it's all right to snack on something fattening between meals because you just won't eat dinner.

Not true.

It is not okay to snack on something fattening between meals and it is not all right to go without dinner. You cannot atone for your own sins.

Jesus Christ is our atonement for sins. You can't atone for

them yourself. As an Overeater Victorious you are learning how
to *eat*, not fast. It may take some struggles and a few ups and
downs, but it's all in the process of getting that flesh of yours
under control. You've been a rebellious person, selfish and un-
committed to the Lord in your eating habits. You're making
progress, but sometimes the going gets a little choppy.

You want to lose weight faster than it wants to get lost. Those
great claims made by promoters of fad diets or weight-loss spas
and clinics, telling you that in thirty days you'll be 30 pounds
thinner, or by Christmas, the Fourth of July, your birthday,
Aunt Maude's housewarming or your own wedding day, you'll be
a sliver of your former fat ugly self, are not only unsound, but unhealthy. We said earlier don't fast to lose weight when you are in
the process of learning how to *eat*. It may throw your whole metabolism out of whack and later you'll gain more weight than
you weigh right now.

Obese people often choose radical weight-loss methods that
harm their bodies and destroy their health because of a mistaken
notion that doing something radical will somehow atone for the
sins that caused them to be fat. Selfishness makes patience hard
to come by.

You want to be 30 pounds slimmer and you want it *now*. The
sooner the better, so naturally, when some promoter comes along
telling you that you can lose a pile of weight in a short time,
you're going to reach into your pocket and pay whatever they ask
to have this dream come true in your life.

The sad thing is, the dream doesn't come true. You may lose
weight, but statistics have shown, if you don't learn new *eating*
habits, the weight doesn't stay off. Don't be like the pathetic
young woman who drank predigested liquid protein and lost 65
pounds, but damaged her heart and metabolism so that she will
never be normal again.

Don't try to atone for your own sins. Jesus is your atonement.
He went to the cross, carrying your fat with Him, so that you
could overcome overeating and be victorious!

Long-suffering

Long-suffering is another fruit of the Spirit. When you think
of long-suffering, you think of patience. Long-suffering is pa-

tience. *Be patient with yourself.* It will take a longer time to get back on your weight-loss program if you condemn yourself. If you have patience and compassion on yourself, you will be able to pick yourself up and start again without wasting too much time in self-pity and condemnation.

You will be able to go from the S in struggle to the Y in victory without the agony of condemnation and guilt.

There is therefore now no condemnation for those who are in Christ Jesus. —Romans 8:1

Remember that.

Long-suffering toward yourself means demonstrating mercy and compassion on yourself. You don't go all to pieces when you blow it; you ask forgiveness and start again. Long-suffering exhibits tolerance, humanity, charity, and tenderness—toward yourself as well as toward others.

Obviously one of the reasons you overeat is that you dislike yourself. You need to fight this lie by being kind to yourself. Whatever you do, reject condemnation.

Jim P. tells how he was once hooked on Pepsi Cola. He drank a minimum of a dozen 12-ounce cans a day. Most of the time he drank more than that. He prayed and prayed for help. He had friends pray for him, too, but nothing seemed to work. He just couldn't break his habit. His stomach, teeth, skin were suffering terribly. He had chronic acne, his teeth were fast decaying and his stomach burned so badly he thought he was getting an ulcer.

Then one day he said, "That's it. This is the last Pepsi I'm drinking," and he gave it up. Within a week, he was feeling better and knew he was rid of the habit forever.

A short time later he began to pray about losing weight. He was 50 pounds overweight. He began the OV program and lost 9 pounds the first week. The weight loss was slower after that and one week he gained 5 pounds. He despaired and sank into a mood of defeat.

"But you conquered the Pepsi habit!" the members of his group reminded him. "You're a success! You're not a failure! Why are you despairing?"

It is so easy to forget our triumphs and concentrate on failure. Long-suffering gives us patience with ourselves.

Jim did not fast to lose the added five pounds and he did not go without lunches for a week, as he wanted to. The weight came off slower than he would have liked, but it came off eventually and permanently.

All discipline for the moment seems not to be joyful, but sorrowful; yet to those who have been trained by it, afterwards it yields the peaceful fruit of righteousness. Therefore, strengthen the hands that are weak and the knees that are feeble, and make straight paths for your feet, so that the limb which is lame may not be put out of joint, but rather be healed. —Hebrews 12:11-13

Maybe this is the first time in your life you've had an opportunity to learn how to be patient with yourself, kind to yourself, gentle to yourself, long-suffering toward yourself. Praise the Lord! It is God's will that you have mercy on yourself. "I will have mercy and not sacrifice," He tells us.

You need long-suffering toward yourself to be a successful Christian. You need it so that if you make a mistake, you don't hate yourself, but you have mercy on yourself.

Prayer

I am a born-again child of God. Thank you, Father, for your great love and mercy. Thank you for sending Jesus to die on the cross so that I don't have to atone for my own sins.

Thank you for your Holy Spirit enabling me to have mastery over my flesh. I refuse to be a selfish person! I have self-control!

Thank you for developing long-suffering and patience in me. Thank you, Lord, for freeing me from self-condemnation. I can be patient, kind and understanding toward myself!

Thank you, Lord, that you do not expect me to conquer all my faults in one day. I am not discouraged at my progress because you are my judge and enabler! PRAISE GOD!

In Jesus' name and for Him. Amen.

sixteen

Look Where You Are!

Bonnie had a great week. She didn't go over her calorie allowance once. She wrote down everything she ate and its calorie content on her log sheet in her notebook. She was so pleased with herself she even started doing physical exercises.

Then she received a jolt of disappointment when she weighed in. Her weight loss for the week was only four ounces!

Talk about discouraging.

Her friend, Linda, had one of the best weeks since beginning her program. She hadn't missed one day's Daily Power Time with Jesus, she recorded her calories faithfully, and she stayed within her calorie allowance perfectly.

When she weighed in she had *gained* a half pound.

Where is justice? you wonder. Both Bonnie and Linda had worked hard, remained faithful (God knows it wasn't easy to say no to little Billy's hardly touched Whopper burger, the rest of Big Bill's milkshake). Is there no reward for such faithful sacrifice?

These girls had a choice, just as you do at times like this when you work hard and don't lose the weight you expected to.

Bonnie and Linda can (1) feel angry, hurt and defeated (all of which cause overeating) or (2) praise the Lord for the victory they won throughout the week by being faithful (which brings you closer to Jesus and gives you a good feeling about yourself).

When you feel good about yourself and the world around you, you don't overeat.

Bonnie and Linda did choose to rejoice. They praised the Lord for the power to remain faithful in spite of temptations and in spite of not losing as much as they hoped to that week. They also praised the Lord that other people had big weight losses that week, and that way they avoided jealousy and frustration.

"I'm victorious!" is the truth they repeatedly said. They knew words like "What's the use? I'm doomed to be fat" were lies.

Do you tell yourself any of the following lies?

____ What's the use? I'm doomed to be fat.

____ I'll never lose weight, no matter how hard I try.

____ I pray, but God doesn't help me.

____ God must be punishing me for my sins. They're too terrible for Him to forgive.

____ I lose weight, but then I gain it right back again. I'll never be thin to stay.

____ God must be sick of my losing weight, gaining it back, and then losing it. Certainly He has lost His patience with me.

All of these statements are lies. Lies! You are *not* doomed to be fat. You *will* lose weight. God *does* help you. Nothing is too terrible for God to forgive! You *will* lose weight and keep it off. God will never lose patience with you. *Trust* Him.

No matter how many times you exceed your calorie allowance or go off your program, God will never give up on you! Start again!

Jeanette is a woman who started her program in the spring, fell off in the summer, started again in the fall, blew it at Christmas, started in January, fell off in April, started again in September; at this writing she's still going strong. She's lost a total of 37 pounds since she began. If she had stuck to her program without falling, she'd be at her goal weight by now, but she is rejoicing at what the Lord is teaching her and doing in her life through her times of stumbling.

You don't overcome that rebellious nature and those rebellious habits overnight.

If you stumble, get up and continue on! Continue on with *Jesus.* Get your nose back into the Bible. Eat your spiritual life-giving food!

In 2 Chronicles 16, it tells how King Asa of Judah went to the king of Syria with gifts of gold and silver, pleading for his help against the king of Israel. The king of Syria obliged and conquered some of Israel's store cities in Naphtali. Then the king of Judah wiped out the work Israel was doing in building Ramah.

It looked like King Asa had really had everything going on his side. He had big armies on his side and he had destroyed the enemy's stronghold. But in the middle of all his victory, God sent a prophet to him who told him, "You really goofed, Asa. God never intended for you to rely on some other king!"

"You mean the king of Syria whom I turned to for help?"

"That's right. God is saying, 'Because you have relied on the king of Syria and have not relied on the Lord your God, you didn't conquer what you were supposed to conquer at all.' "

King Asa didn't like what he was hearing. He had a rebellious heart. He wanted to do things *his* way.

"Asa, listen to me," the prophet continued. "The eyes of the Lord move to and fro throughout the earth that He may strongly support those whose heart is completely His. You have acted foolishly in this."

Why do we turn to fad diets, fasts, pills, drugs, shots, liquid drinks, powdered drinks, occult practices to lose weight? These all fail before they begin. *God does not fail.*

Asa sounds like a familiar character. (We may wonder if he had a weight problem!) He wanted to depend on *himself* and his own ways and not on God.

What usually happens when you trust yourself and not God? If you fail, you get angry. That's what Asa did. He got furious. He threw the prophet in jail and took his wrath out on some of the people.

He didn't want to win his battles God's way. He didn't want God's power and God's overcoming strength. He wanted *his* way. (Our way is to eat whatever and whenever we want with nobody to get in our way.)

King Asa could have repented and started over again. But he didn't. He refused to repent. (That's what a long food binge is like. After the first ten minutes, each additional mouthful of food is a refusal to repent.) Asa absolutely refused to repent and start again with the Lord.

So he failed—and failed miserably at that. He became diseased in his feet and in verse 12 it says his disease was really severe. But even *then* he wouldn't turn to the Lord for help. Do you know whom he turned to? Some physicians. That's like some obese people who are so sick with obesity that they overeat even more. (See chapter seventeen, "Why Do You Overeat?")

No matter how slow the weight loss is, don't give up. Even if you gain weight, don't give up. Many people will lose weight and then gain some, but if you stick with it, you'll lose more than you gained and you'll be nearer your goal.

You are at a very important place in your life. See Ephesians 1:3-14 and look where you are.

Blessed be the God and Father of our Lord Jesus Christ, who has blessed us with every spiritual blessing in the heavenly places in Christ.

You are blessed not only with one or two little blessings, but with *every* spiritual blessing in heavenly places in Christ. When you're with Christ, you are in heavenly places, whether standing at the door of the refrigerator or on your knees in prayer. Your heart and your mind belong to Him to bless with *every* spiritual blessing. His spiritual blessings are eternal. They are heavenly. You are not hopeless, or a failure in Christ. You are *blessed.*

Just as He chose us in Him before the foundation of the world that we should be holy and blameless before Him.

You are chosen! You aren't a person sitting on the fringe of the heavenly parade wishing you could be a part of it. You *are* in there! You're *chosen!*

In love He predestined us to adoption as sons (daughters, too) through Jesus Christ to Himself, according to the kind intention of His will.

You are adopted by Him. He has picked you to father, to take care of, to raise and love. His intentions toward you are loving and kind.

To the praise of the glory of His grace, which He freely bestowed on us in the Beloved.

You are lavished in His grace, in His unfailing and unmerited mercy!

In Him we have redemption through His blood, the forgiveness of our trespasses, according to the riches of His grace.

Do you know what it is to be forgiven?—really forgiven? Forgiven for every second and third helping your body didn't need, every gorging and binging experience? Do you know what it is to be forgiven for the causes of your overeating?

Have you prayed, "Dear Lord, *forgive* me for these feelings of frustration"? or "the mistaken notion that life is passing me by, and I'm missing out on happiness and beauty"?

Riches in grace mean rich in forgiveness, renewing, healing, restoring, blessing. Redemption means to be bought back from the rightful owner. We have redemption through the blood He bled when He was hung on the cross and we're forgiven!

Which He lavished upon us. In all wisdom and insight.

You're no dummy. You have wisdom and insight! Use it!

He made known to us the mystery of His will, according to His kind intention which He purposed in Him.

(Listen, if you think you just can't figure out what God's will is for you, read this verse again.) He has made the mystery of His will known to us! It says so right here. Take it. Pray, "Lord, I take the power to know the mystery of your will just as it says in this ninth verse of Ephesians 1."

Also we have obtained an inheritance, having been predestined according to His purpose who works all things after the counsel of His will.

Oh, that's good news. Do you know what it is to receive an inheritance? That means somebody *gives* you something; you inherit it. If you had a distant uncle who left you a million dollars in his will, you'd be pretty excited when that check arrived, wouldn't you? The inheritance you have in the Lord so far exceeds money or riches.

—to the end that we who were the first to hope in Christ should be to the praise of His glory.

We are the praise of His glory. You can choose to be a powerful and impressive praise to His glory. You can be a self-controlled, long-suffering Overeater Victorious to the praise of His glory. You can lose pounds and inches to the praise of His glory. You can remain faithful to your eating program no matter how long it seems to take to lose weight to the *praise of His glory.*

In Him, you also, after listening to the message of truth, the gospel of your salvation—having also believed, you were sealed in Him with the Holy Spirit of promise.

You're not just tacked onto Jesus with a straight pin or a paper clip. You're not just attached to the promises of heaven with scotch tape or thumbtacks. You're *sealed* in Jesus. You're sealed with the Holy Spirit of promise. There's no greater sealer than the Holy Spirit. He is eternal, all powerful, all knowing, wise and wonderful.

Who is given as a pledge of our inheritance, with a view to the redemption of God's own possession, to the praise of His glory.

You are God's own possession. You're sealed into Him and you are His possession.

And all this time you thought you were worthless?

Reread the above verses. Write your own paraphrases and memorize them. This is your position in Christ. You are above your circumstance. You are no longer a victim of circumstances. You're blessed with every spiritual blessing in heavenly places. Ephesians 2:6 says that you are raised up with Him, seated with Him in heavenly places. You're above it all!

Start acting on what you are in Him.

Walking with Jesus Every Day

Here is what we might look like on a scale when we are walking with Jesus every day. We are endeavoring to lose weight, to be more like Him, to yield every area of our lives over to Him, to rise above all struggles and difficulties with His overcoming wisdom and strength, to trust Him for all things and to live as truly blessed people in heavenly places in Christ.

And, we don't do it all in a day. Galatians 5:24 reads, "Those who belong to Christ Jesus have crucified the flesh with its passions and desires." This means it has been done already.

Our problem is to live like it's been done. Is that old passion of yours for ice cream or pizza still raging strong within you? This verse says if you belong to Christ, you have already crucified your old godless nature and all those old ugly passions for destructive eating. Now the thing to do is to live like it.

Prayer

In the name of Jesus, I renounce my old carnal nature. The godless passions and desires in my life are no longer going to have a hold over me. I know that they are crucified! Crucified with Christ because I am His! My mind is His, my will is His, my thoughts are His, my desires are His, my passions are His, my heart is His, my needs are His, my wants are His.

I am blessed in every spiritual blessing in heavenly places in Christ!

I am *chosen* in Him before the foundation of the world!

I am predestined as an *adopted* person of His!

I am lavished in His *grace*!

I have *redemption* through His blood and *forgiveness*!

I have *wisdom* and *insight* in the name of Jesus!

He has made the mystery of *His will* known to His children!

I have obtained an *inheritance* in Christ!

I am *sealed* in Him with the Holy Spirit of promise!

I AM GOD'S OWN POSSESSION!

In the mighty name of Jesus, Amen.

seventeen

Why Do You Overeat?

For years Shirley R. blamed her overeating on her husband. If he weren't such an impossible person with so many problems, she said, she wouldn't be nervous and frustrated and wouldn't eat so much.

Jim D., a college student, blamed his overeating on the pressures of school. He said he could hardly wait until he graduated so he could get his eating under control. (Three weeks after graduation he put on ten more pounds. He blamed it on boredom.)

Connie S. gained 15 pounds after her divorce. Tom K. gained 20 pounds when he was switched to another department at his place of work. Lorraine T. gained 70 pounds with her pregnancy. Marcia D. gained 30 pounds after her husband died. Every year at vacation time Darlene L. gains from 5 to 10 pounds. Blames it on her children who, although thin, love to eat.

Why do *you* overeat?

Have you ever thought your problem was unique and separate from the rest of the world? If your thin friends had the life of troubles that you had, they'd gain weight, too, you think.

Have you ever thought nobody suffers like you do? This way of thinking says everybody has a happier and better life than you and eating is all you've got. The notion that others are happier, better off and leading lives of comparative ease is not true at all. There is also a mistaken belief that it's not as hard for others to lose weight as it is for you. Everyone who has ever gone on a weight-loss program has had to struggle with temptation, deny themselves and go without.

That's what it says in the Word anyhow. In 1 Corinthians 10:13 it says:

No temptation has overtaken you but such as is common to man.

This verse is telling us that we are in a human realm of existence and the problems that beset us are all within this human realm. There's no superhuman task for us to undertake when we are within the confines of this realm. That's why the Lord tells us in Matthew 17:20 that if we have the faith as a grain of a mustard seed, nothing is impossible to us.

There is not a single temptation that is beyond human resistance.

> . . . and God is faithful, who will not allow you to be tempted beyond what you are able, but with the temptation will provide the way of escape also, that you may be able to endure it.— 1 Corinthians 10:13

With the temptation God always provides a way of escaping its power over you so that you may endure and not fall.

The reason many of us don't grab hold of this promise is because we want to be excused from our Christian responsibility to think and act like Christians.

What Makes Us Do It?

Has anyone or anything made you angry lately? Anyone or anything made you upset, worried, furious, miserable, frustrated, depressed or anxious?

Have you ever noticed the way children behave when they've been caught doing something they shouldn't be doing? One of the first things they might say is, "Oh, he/she made me do it!" Two small boys invade the cookie jar and when Mother happens on the scene, they both point at the other and say in harmony, "*He* made me do it!"

It's the mature person who can stop blaming people and situations for his/her own sins. The responsibility for our happiness is on our own shoulders. Nobody else holds it for us. We do.

People don't actually *make* you angry. You make yourself angry. Imagine driving in your car with a friend. This friend is telling you every turn and stop to make, as if you had never been behind a wheel before. He is being a backseat driver *par excellence.*

You think to yourself, "This guy is really making me angry. In a minute I'll explode."

Explode you may, but not because he makes you angry. You may want to throw your Indie 500 trophy at him, as well as your international chauffeur's license, but please, as you do, say the truth and tell him, "I *make myself* angry when you tell me how to drive."

Nobody else *makes* you anything. You make *yourself* feel, think, say, act and do what you do. Nobody else actually makes you overeat. You overeat because of you.

You *condition* yourself to eat what you eat, where you eat, how much you eat and when you eat.

What It Means To Be Conditioned

If you have had several happy experiences eating and watching TV, there is an automatic trigger inside your brain that will tell you *eat* when you get in front of the TV. You only need to see a TV set turned on and you'll feel like eating something. If you have paperwork to do and you've conditioned yourself to eat while working, you'll find yourself thinking of food as you work. If you have made a habit of eating when you're depressed, upset, lonely or worried, your brain will tell you *eat* when you are in these states of mind. You've conditioned yourself to eat when you encounter these stressful circumstances.

Now, here's the good news. You can de-condition yourself. You can develop new habits so that your brain does not think *food* when you are in certain situations or places or engaging in certain activities. One woman says that she doesn't overeat at all during the day when she is on the job, but the minute she walks into her apartment, she starts to eat and doesn't stop until she goes to bed.

Somewhere along the line she conditioned herself to think food and home are inseparable. On the job she didn't think about eating, but once home, her "eat" trigger was pushed and off she went, eating everything in sight.

Home should not mean food to us. Home is a million things, and eating is only one of the things we do there. Those experiences as a child when Mother cooked up those feasts in her kitchen and all the family rallied around the table for family time, with food as the main attraction, may still remain in your memory. So you spend your years trying to relive these childhood experiences. Or maybe relaxation means food to you. When you arrive home after a day of pressure and hard work, you want to relax. Relaxation means food, so you not only eat, but you overeat.

You can end these lifetime patterns and develop new ones. You re-condition yourself.

Check if you do any of the following:

- Eat while watching TV
- Eat while driving the car.
- Eat while studying or doing paperwork.
- Eat while reading.
- Eat while on the job.
- Eat while shopping.
- Eat while preparing a meal.
- Eat when cleaning up after a meal.
- Eat more alone than with others.
- Eat before going to bed.
- Get out of bed in the middle of the night to eat.
- Eat more on weekends than during the week.
- Eat more at night than during the day.
- Skip breakfast but gorge later on in the day.

Many books on dieting will tell you to substitute those fattening snacks you've been eating during these times for low-cal snacks. This is acceptable, but it is not breaking the patterns that have been set up in your response system. If you really want mastery over these habits in your life, end them.

Don't eat while watching TV. (Do your nails, sew, whittle, carve or paint something instead.)

Don't eat while driving the car. (Wait until you get to a restaurant, home, or wait until a certain time.)

Don't eat while studying or doing paperwork. (A glass of water will be terrific.)

Don't eat while reading. (Be good to yourself. Enjoy your book without getting fat.)

Don't eat while on the job. (Wait until lunch or dinner and reward yourself with thinness.)

Don't eat while shopping. (Your body will love you for it.)

Don't eat while preparing a meal. (Your body doesn't want you to put more into it than it needs.)

Don't eat while cleaning up after a meal. (You are not a garbage disposal; you are a beautiful human being.)

Don't eat more alone than when you're with others. (Be good to yourself at all times, not just in front of others.)

Don't get out of bed in the middle of the night to eat. (Your stomach deserves a rest.)

Don't eat before going to bed. (Think beautiful thoughts instead and have a Jesus snack in the Word.)

Don't eat more on weekends than during the week. (Discover your "triggers" and put an end to them.)

Don't eat more at night than during the day. (Do something fun instead of eating.)

Don't skip breakfast and gorge at other times. (Breakfast is energy time. You are too special to go without your a.m. energy.)

The only danger in substituting carrots for potato chips as a snack is that you may eat carrots for a while, but then go back to potato chips again. The habit hasn't been dealt with. If you end the habit, you've gotten to the source of things.

You may have a string of Freudian excuses for overeating and being fat, but these don't have to keep you fat. You can change your behavior if you really want to. It doesn't matter what your mother fed you when you were just a tot, or what you went without as an adolescent, or what your family eating patterns were. You can say NO to those old habits and stop analyzing and making excuses for them.

God says He will *provide a way of escape* for you. If you are a compulsive eater, God will *provide a way of escape.* If you are an impulsive eater, God will *provide a way of escape.* That's what it says in 1 Corinthians 10:13. He is right now providing a way of escape for you if you will take it.

Practical Helps for Those Tough Times of Temptation

1. Tell your friends you're on a special eating program when they invite you for dinner. Tell them exactly what you *may* eat and what you may not. Don't use this opportunity to binge. Your friends will be happy to cooperate when they see it is important to you.

2. When you eat in a restaurant, do not examine the menu. Plan what you'll order before you get there. Think of the many lovely foods you can plan your meal from. A large salad with strips of turkey and cheese; cottage cheese; lean meat; chicken without the skin; broiled fish with no butter; a baked potato with no butter; fresh fruit. Don't use eating out as an ex-

cuse to binge. Remember, you are a very special person. You deserve to be good to yourself.

3. Other people may not have yielded their eating habits to the Lord yet. Don't worry yourself about them. You be the obedient one and praise the Lord you are. If others want to eat fattening and unhealthy foods, you don't have to join them. You eat your salad and broiled fish and thank Jesus you've taken the escape He has provided for you!

4. Count your calories. Count them *before* you eat them. Be in control of things.

5. Don't buy fattening junk foods. If your family insists on these foods, let them buy them. One woman told her husband, "Those snacks and junk foods will have to come out of the entertainment money because my grocery money must go for *food.*"

6. Cut up carrots, celery and cauliflower immediately and keep in a plastic container in the refrigerator to have some ready healthy "fast food" on hand.

7. At church dinners, potlucks, showers, weddings and other food-oriented activities, pack your own nutritious and scrumptious eats in plastic containers and bags. Slip into the kitchen and put your food on a plate like the others have— things like fresh fruit with lemon dressing, cold sliced turkey, shredded cheese, crisp vegetable salad. Carry a thermos of mint tea or another herb tea so you don't have to put Kool-Aid or some sugary punch into your body.

8. You don't have to substitute chemical sweeteners for sugar. You don't have to put the artificial sweeteners in your precious body. You don't have to drink artificially sweetened sodas or drinks. You can use honey and maple syrup as sweeteners and for your cooking and baking needs, and eat plenty of fresh fruit. Drink fresh fruit juices without sugar. Praise the Lord for your health and beauty.

You are a unique and special person—a very important person. You deserve to have good things. Those good things do *not* include fattening and harmful foods.

You are His workmanship, created in Christ Jesus for good works (Eph. 2:10). You are unique as a person created with His very own hands. He loves your soul, your spirit *and your body.*

He knows your body. He formed you. It's important to Him that it operate and function well.

> *For thou didst form my inward parts;*
> *Thou didst weave me in my mother's womb.*
> *I will give thanks to Thee, for I am fearfully and wonderfully made;*
> *Wonderful are Thy works,*
> *And my soul knows it very well.*
> *My frame was not hidden from Thee,*
> *When I was made in secret,*
> *And skillfully wrought in the depths of the earth.* —Psalm 139: 13-15

You have begun your weight-loss program and you're going to lose every ounce you intend to lose. Remember that. You're going to stick with it no matter how long it takes. There may be a million temptations, but He is continually providing a way of escape for you. The Word of God will take first place over the thing you're tempted to eat. You'll speak the Word to yourself and love it far more than that thing you almost ate.

The Lord will accomplish that which concerns me (Ps. 138:8) is your promise and your strength.

You are unique and special, and your problems are human. They are the same problems and struggles we all face. You are *never* alone when you are losing weight.

You are never alone when you are exercising self-control. Somebody else right now is saying no to dessert, too. Someone else right now has found that way the Lord provides the overeater for escape—as you are discovering.

Prayer

Dearest Lord, thank you that you did give me a way of escape from overeating. Thank you, Lord, that those things which trigger off an overeating response in me can be ENDED!

Give me the power and strength to change my overeating habits in the name of Jesus! I choose to change my overeating habits now. I receive the Lord's means of escape from (name the overeating habits you've been a victim of) in the name of Jesus!

I am free from fat! I am free to be the real me as God ordained me to be free to be thin! In Jesus' name, Amen.

eighteen

Who Says You Have to Overeat?

Elizabeth has raised a family of four boys. She, her husband and the boys are all overweight. One of her sons couldn't get into the army because of his obesity and another one was turned down for a job he wanted. (More and more companies are discovering obesity a health hazard and won't hire fat people.) Elizabeth broke into tears as she told how she had been deceived for years, thinking she was a good wife and mother by serving her family rich and fattening foods. She baked fresh breads and pastries nearly every week. She spent long hours in the kitchen cooking heavy, fattening meals. Actually she cooked these foods because *she* liked them. Through the years she taught her family how to like them and reinforced these likes by continuing to cook the same way, establishing a life-style of wrong eating for six people.

Not only was she creating a health hazard, but also a fast-growing social concern.

Drs. Bruch Hannon and Timothy Lohman, two scientists from the University of Illinois at Urbana, say that Americans should be alerted to the energy output it takes to supply more food than overweight people need.

Their research has shown that the excess energy used to feed America's fat people could supply the annual residential electrical needs of Boston, Chicago, San Francisco and Washington, D.C.

Their figures, from a variety of federal agencies and other studies, show that if all overweight adults simultaneously went on diets to reach their optimum weights, the energy saved during the three to four-month diet period would be equivalent to 1.3 billion gallons of gasoline.

Being overweight is a social problem and not only a personal concern, according to the scientists.

If Americans weighed the optimum weight and no more, the annual energy savings would equal three-quarters of a billion gallons of gasoline, enough to run more than 900,000 cars each year or to supply the electrical needs of four metropolitan centers. These calculations are based on the amount of fossil fuel energy required to supply the extra food calories to maintain excess body fat on overweight people.

According to these studies, Elizabeth was stuffing her family's bellies and adding to the energy crisis without ever realizing what she was doing.

One of the first fears she expressed in her OV group concerned dieting and how it would affect her state of mind. She was afraid she'd be nervous, tense or easily-irritated if she didn't eat the foods she was accustomed to.

That's another misconception. Being stuffed does not make you healthier or happier.

Nutrition and Mental Health

What you eat plays an important role in your emotional state of being. You may be fat and consuming huge amounts of food, but if you are not getting the vitamins and minerals your body requires according to your life-style, metabolism and body needs, you will suffer for it.

A common contributor to unnecessary weight gain is lack of understanding. If you are not conscious of food values, calorie content and nutritional benefits, you will not only remain fat, but you may be doing serious harm to your body and mind. The measure of your success is not only in losing weight, but in *keeping it off and having a healthy mind and body.*

If you are subject to periods of depression, mental confusion and other emotional deviations for which you find no psychological cause, you may want to examine your diet. Evaluate what you are eating and see if you are eating a *high-protein, moderate-carbohydrate* diet necessary for optimum mental stability. Are you getting enough B vitamins (tension reducing), potassium (easily excreted during stress periods), magnesium (vital for control of muscle tension and irritability)?

Processed cereals, white flour, white sugar do not offer the complete range of B vitamins necessary to promote adequate food metabolism. Coffee and other caffeine beverages stimulate the insulin production and cover up fatigue. Avoid them because they hide the symptoms of low blood sugar and detract its cure. These are some of the foods that stand in the way of mental health.

Exercise—What's That?

It's nothing new that overweight people don't particularly love to exercise. One obese man sat in his chair watching the rain leak through the ceiling for hours before he got up to do something about it. "Just didn't feel like moving," he explained. He said he could sit for hours in one place, hardly moving, while his thin wife would get cramps sitting still so long.

It isn't hard to understand why an overweight person doesn't like to exercise. It's laborious moving around a lot of extra pounds of weight. For some people, it hurts! A fat person gets tired before a thin person does. He has less stamina and resistance to fatigue.

A fat person burns up more calories doing the same amount of exercise as a thin person, because it takes more energy for him to move his extra weight. That's why grossly overweight persons lose weight faster than persons less overweight.

Your body has 666 skeletal muscles. Each muscle loves to be worked. Bless your muscles by using them. You don't have to work out every day on the jogging trail, the gym and tennis court, but touching your toes once in a while wouldn't hurt anything. A few windmills with your arms swinging back and forth wouldn't be too demanding a couple of times a day. And a few stretches from the waist might be fun once in a while.

You don't have to overdo it.

A little at a time and easy does it are your rules of thumb. Overweight people are more discouraged than inspired by the demands of physical exercise. Ask the Lord how much you should be exercising and what kind of exercises you should be doing.

You may want to take a daily half-hour walk. Or bicycle a half hour a day. Perhaps joining a health spa or gym would be just the thing for you. The Holy Spirit is your guide and He won't fail you.

One thing you can count on: God won't wear you out and

have you racked with pain and misery from overdoing it. He loves your body and wants you to learn how to take good care of it.

Lack of exercise and weight gain can result in a sense of low self-esteem and depression. When your self-esteem is low and you feel depressed, you reach for the high-calorie undesirable foods. It's a vicious cycle.

Doctors agree that proper nutrition, adequate rest and physical exercise are needed for optimum health. Diseases caused by insufficient physical activity include obesity.

A common misbelief is that exercise or physical activity will increase the appetite. The truth is that Americans, on the whole, are already overeating for their energy needs. Research studies have proven that food intake actually declines as people move from low to moderate activity occupations. Strenuous exercise before a meal frequently acts to decrease appetite. Also, if exercise in a regular form is enjoyable, it will replace the inappropriate eating brought on by boredom and tension.

Most people don't relish the idea of exercising for weight loss because it takes so much to lose so little. It certainly isn't inspiring to know that you'd have to run up and down the stairs of the Empire State Building for four hours to lose one pound of body fat. Who needs it?

The rule of thumb again is *slow and easy*. Don't get yourself discouraged. A little at a time is fine! Instead of a four-hour running marathon up and down the steps of the Empire State Building, try something easier. Like walking to the store instead of riding (that is, if you don't live eight miles from the nearest store). Or running in place for 30 seconds a couple of times a day. Easy!

A person could lose nine pounds a year just by climbing the stairs to his/her fourth-floor office and back down four times a day.

If you are inactive, you must rigidly control your calorie intake or you will gain weight quickly. If you exercise moderately and regularly, you will not only feel better, but you'll be using up more calories.

Be good to yourself! The next time a friend suggests going out for a cup of coffee, convince them to go for a walk with you instead.

Instead of making your nights out centered around a restaurant and eating, do something active like bowling, swimming, walking, jogging or playing volley ball, tennis, golf, basketball, pingpong, badminton. If you don't know how to do any of these things, learn. You are in charge of your circumstances. You create your own circumstances. If you've never played golf and you go for your first lesson feeling terribly self-conscious and unhappy about all the exercise involved, just tell yourself it may be difficult now, but it won't be when you're thinner. You're getting ready for that day now by learning how to do fun physical activities. You'll stay thin when you have a variety of activities to do with your new thin body.

If you live in the city and are discovering that exercise costs money, you can find cheap ways of getting physical activity. Walking and jogging are free. If you decide to jog, do it along a route where lots of other people jog. There you'll see many overweight people jogging away for fitness and health and you won't feel self-conscious. You don't have to be a track star to jog.

Walking is just as beneficial as jogging. It just takes longer to get where you're going. Walking is something you can do for free and it's great fun. Swing your arms, walk briskly, breathe deeply. Ah, yes, you'll wonder why you didn't do it sooner.

If your mailbox is at the end of your driveway, run instead of walk to it each day to pick up your mail.

While waiting for your spin-cycle on the washing machine to finish, run in place for a half minute or so.

When driving the car or sitting at your desk, hold your stomach in for a count of twenty. Release and do it again. Do that a few times a day.

Another good exercise is to avoid using the elevator if you can walk. Stand on tiptoes and then lower your heels, up and down, up and down, five or ten times a few times a day. Fun!

You don't have to be an Olympic champion to be thin and in shape. You don't have to be "the athletic type" to enjoy a couple of physical activities that will bless your body. (How many times have you heard an overweight person shrug off exercise by saying, "I'm just not the athletic type"?)

One of the main excuses for avoiding physical exercise is that we think exercise means lifting weights at the gym, strenuous calisthenics or some other laborious and enervating activity.

EASY is the word. Take it EASY and enjoy your exercise. Be like the 40-year-old woman who started doing deep breathing exercises at the same time she started her weight-loss program. As the weight fell off, she added a few more exercises. By the time she reached her goal weight (a loss of 30 pounds), she was in better shape than when she was a teenager active in sports.

If you start slowly and if you do exercises that you enjoy, you can add more as your weight drops. Pray about the amount of exercise you get. Are you exercising your precious body enough?

Prayer

Dear Lord, my body needs exercise. Show me how much exercise to do and what kinds to do. I want to be a good steward of this body. I want to take care of it the best way I can. I want it to feel good, to be strong and to have plenty of energy.

I choose to exercise to the glory of God. I choose to take care of this body for the glory of God!

Now, dear Lord, give me the grace to bring you glory and honor through this body you have given me.

My life belongs to you, Lord, and I choose this day to exercise my body for you.

In Jesus' name, Amen.

nineteen

Reaching Your Goal and the Maintenance Program

It was for freedom that Christ set us free; therefore keep standing firm and do not be subject again to a yoke of slavery.—Galatians 5:1

Five women stand at the front of the room, smiling and wearing their Overeaters Victorious "I Made It" pins. Among them they have lost nearly 200 pounds.

Sally says, "I can't tell you how happy I am to at last be able to get into the back seat of a two-door car. That's something I couldn't do before. I was too fat."

Karen says, "At last I can wear something with a waistline. And I can wear slacks. I was always too fat to wear slacks so I wore tent dresses. Now I can wear pant suits and not look like a basketball."

"I used to have to buy men's clothes," says Terry. "Men's clothes were bigger and made me feel smaller. I could get a medium in men's clothes, but in women's clothing I was an extra large."

Bonnie added: "I wore a bathing suit for the first time in ten years this week. If I ever went to the beach I wore cutoffs and a tee-shirt because I felt too fat to wear a bathing suit. Thank God those days are over!" Gloria tells of her delight when she was able to take off her coat. "I wore a coat *all* the time. In church I never took it off. I wore a coat even if the weather wasn't cold. Thank God, I can take it off now."

They share how they carried large purses in front of them to hide their fat, how they couldn't sit on a folding chair or cross their knees, they were unable to bend over or wear clothing with zippers.

The Greatest Victory

What could be better than being thin? many overweight people ask. What could be better than being able to sit cross-legged on the floor and then get up again without rolling over and flapping like a porpoise? What could be better than throwing out the tent dresses and size 24-1/2 pant suits? What could be better than buying a pair of blue jeans and looking like a teenager when you're in your thirties?

Here's what five women said.

Kay: "I'm so happy to be thin I can hardly stand it! But truthfully, my greatest victory was not just in losing weight. My real victory was the one over self and my own selfish desires. I've been a selfish and demanding person all my life. I demanded from people, from God and from life. Everybody *else* was supposed to make me happy. Oh, the change in me has been great. My husband says he can hardly believe I'm the same person. He says it's like having a new wife. See, when I didn't get my own way, I'd get angry. I was angry *all* the time. And when I was angry, I ate. All the wrong foods, naturally. Losing 57 pounds is wonderful, and through losing all that weight I've become a new person."

Ann: "I used to be aggressive and loud. I used to think I was bold, but really, I was being pushy. I always felt driven to do something, be something, gain recognition, get people's attention and love. Now people are telling me they can't get over the change in me. I honestly feel a real sense of self-respect and inner contentment which I've never had before in my whole life. I know it's because of what God has done in me while losing weight."

Jeanine: "I know what you mean. I had so many problems that manifested themselves through overeating. God showed me that my overweight was not a problem that stood alone. It was due largely to my rebellion against accepting His will in my life. I wanted my way, He wanted His. Guess who loses in a tug-of-war like that! I lose if I don't obey, that's for sure. I win if I obey. I decided to obey. It wasn't easy at times. Often I thought I was being tortured needlessly and I wanted to eat something I wasn't supposed to. But I stuck to the program and now I've reached my goal. I feel better now than I have in my whole life!"

Gloria: "Every day for one year I counted each and every calorie that went into my mouth. I didn't miss a single bite. I wrote down every calorie. I followed the program perfectly. I lost 81-1/2 pounds. Now, a year may seem like a long time to count calories, but staying at my goal weight is not hard for me because I spent a whole year developing new habits and attitudes about food. The Lord has shown me how possessive and unruly I was. My life was filled with lack of discipline and rebellion. I didn't even know it! I wanted, wanted, wanted. I was angry, hostile, spoiled, grouchy—you name it. I cry every time I think of how God has gotten rid of all that old garbage in my life. He did more than clean out my stomach. He cleaned out my heart and soul as well."

It was for freedom that Christ set us free; therefore keep standing firm and do not be subject again to a yoke of slavery.—Galatians 5:1

Ethel Waters, in her biography, *To Me It's Wonderful,* talks about her battle with fat. She was more than 200 pounds overweight and had lost her ability to do even ordinary things like walk or sit in a chair and get up again. Being obese had made her bitter, also. She hated being fat, hated herself for being fat and hated others for reminding her she was fat.

It's no fun to be so fat that everyday activities become enormous obstacles to overcome. It's hard on the self-esteem when the safety belts in cars and airplanes won't go around you. Ethel Waters was humiliated and horrified when a plane she was on actually had to delay take-off until an extension belt was found long enough to go around her. When she sang in concerts she had to wear the microphone around her neck because she couldn't get close enough to a standing microphone. Her stomach was too big. She said, "Don't laugh at a fatty. They're *handicapped.*"

"If you're fat," she said, "get it off, or it can kill you. I know." She lost *200 pounds* by faithfully following her doctor's orders and praying to her heavenly Father for help. As she lost weight, she lost the bitterness and anger, too. Her love for God and people grew and she became one of the most beloved Christian performers of all time. She was already a brilliant performer and famous all over the world, but she went on to become one of the most well-loved *Christian* performers of all time.

Overeating for whatever reason you can think of is a *bondage.* It's like being in a prison or being wrapped in heavy chains from head to toe. You're trapped like an animal in a cage, unable to move in freedom. Binging and gluttony are your slave drivers. They crack the whip and you jump like a beaten and wretched slave. Whatever emotion you blame your overeating on, you are a slave to it. You may say, "Oh dear, I'm feeling depressed. I want to *eat* a little something."

Or, "How dare he speak to me that way. He doesn't love me. Nobody loves me. I'm all alone in this life, loveless and lonely. I think I'll eat."

Thoughts like these shove you right into the prison cell and shut the doors behind you. You're caught. In goes the food and out goes your stomach. Soon your stomach sticks out farther than your chest and soon you can't sit with your legs together anymore. Soon you find you can't be comfortable leaning back in a straight chair; you have to straddle it like riding horseback. You're uncomfortable in a school desk and you can't wear seatbelts. You're hooked, trapped and whipped. You are indeed "handicapped."

Who needs it? Now that you've reached the Maintenance Program, you've arrived home at last. Your body has finally emerged from that hulk you once were. The real you has popped out of those prison walls. Thank God, you're free! It was for the sake of freedom that your Savior set you free. Praise God, keep standing firm! Don't go back to that ugly prison again!

You have victoriously feasted on Jesus and His Word and reached your goal weight. The real you is now reading these words. Those hands of yours are no longer swollen and bulging around your rings, your breathing is easier and you aren't gasping for breath. Your clothes fit. You feel great. Praise God, you're the real you! You are free to be thin!

Many of the OV losers have said, "That fat person just wasn't me. I knew somewhere in all those extra pounds there was a real me!"

Who Goes on Maintenance?

You go on the Maintenance Program when you reach the *spiritual goals* that God has set for you. This is the point where you are utterly honest with the Lord in your life. You no longer hide calories from the Lord, you don't miss your Daily Power Time, you fight those things that trigger gluttonous eating, you stop complaining about not being able to eat certain foods, you remain faithful to your calling and God's will for your body.

If you are still having temper tantrums and going on weekend binges, you aren't ready for the maintenance program quite yet. *You want to maintain the good work God has done in you for the rest of your life.* You don't want to prolong the fleshly indulgences and poor habits.

Purpose of the Maintenance Program

The reason we go on the Maintenance Program is so that God can continue to move in our lives, as He desires. God has a lot He wants done in our lives and He wants to get on with it! The longer you sit in fleshly indulgences, self-pity, anger, overeating, gluttony, binging, gorging and eating wrong foods, the longer it takes Him to get on with the other wonderful things He has for you in your life! DON'T MISS OUT!

Maintaining your goal weight is God's method of keeping control of your actions and desires. You must never take this away from Him.

When you begin your maintenance program there are two things that will be different at first.

1. You will not be counting calories in the same way any longer.

Keeping the calorie log has become second nature to most of us. The successful losers on the OV program are so used to counting calories, it's hard to stop.

But you don't stop entirely. Once you reach your ideal weight and you are at the spiritual level of obedience that God wants you, you count calories two days a week—on Mondays and Fridays. On the other days, you write in your log MAINTENANCE. Some people notice they actually eat *less* when they ease off the calorie logs. It's because they're completely at the mercy of God and depending on Him to guide and direct them.

If you can't make it without counting calories, by all means continue on. The idea is to *slowly* wean off the calorie log sheets. Don't do it all at once! If recording Monday and Friday is uncomfortable, start by eliminating just one day a week. Write

MAINTENANCE under that day. You have self-control now. A person with self-control is ready to go on a weight maintenance program.

"But how do I know what to eat?" you may ask. You *do* know what to eat. You have been on the program long enough and listened to the voice of the Lord long enough and been in the Word long enough to know very well what to eat and what not to eat. *Stand firm and do not be subject again to a yoke of slavery.* You are now accustomed to saying NO to your own fleshly indulgence and saying YES to the Holy Spirit when He guides you in godly eating.

Ask the Lord if, what and how much you may eat. When you ask Him how many calories you ought to eat, He may very well answer you, "You know what your body needs. I already taught you that."

The reason you are on the Maintenance Program now is that you *do* understand yourself and your body and you are in *control.* Imagine spending several weeks teaching a child how to ride a bicycle. He falls a few times, makes some errors, but finally, he does very well. He gains coordination and stays up on the bicycle. You can see that he has learned how to ride well. Then you tell him, "Okay, you're ready to go on that bike trip."

He answers, "But how do I ride the bike?"

You answer, "I taught you how to ride. You know how to ride. All you have to do is *do it* now."

"But how do I do it? What do I need to know in order to ride the bicycle?"

"I already told you everything you need to know. You already showed me that you know how to ride the bike. You are prepared. Go ahead."

Your calorie limit is now removed. By now you *know* how many calories it takes to maintain your weight. (See chapter twenty-two.)

The reason God wants you to act on what you know is that He wants to teach you something new! He doesn't want you in the same old ruts forever. You have learned much about yourself and your body. Now go on! He has much more for you!

Every day when you get out of bed, ask the Lord what you should eat that day. Give Him your day and every morsel of food you'll be putting into your mouth.

The three big questions you ask Him are:
1. May I eat?
2. May I eat _____ ? (Name the foods)
3. How *much* may I eat?

Don't make God a liar when you ask Him what He wants you to eat. If you're sitting in a restaurant and the glass case with the revolving pies is within eyesight, don't say to the Lord, "May I have that ugly disgusting pie?" and then, because you're hungry, answer yourself, "Why certainly, go right ahead. It only has 400 ugly, disgusting calories. But you don't need to worry. You're on maintenance now!"

You're on maintenance and all the more reason to STAND FIRM. Pie should be no less disgusting to you now than it was while you were losing weight. Neva Coyle didn't taste ice cream for two years. "This is a lifetime thing," she explains. "Things like candy and ice cream are no friends of mine. They aren't *treats*, either, I'll tell you that. They are *enemies*. I don't consider cakes and cookies *refreshments* either. Not when you were once 248 pounds. These foods are threats to my health and well-being. I choose to stand firm and not be subject again to the yoke of slavery these kinds of 'refreshments' and 'treats' once had on me. My treats are now healthy, life-giving foods, the kind my body loves, like fresh fruit, yogurt, raw vegetables and fresh juices."

2. You will have a closer awareness of yourself through your journal.

Keep a very close log of your feelings, moods, behavior at this time. Make your journal entries longer and spend more time in the Scriptures. The reason for this is that you need to have complete control over yourself, your desires, thoughts, wants, dreams, emotions and actions. Leave nothing to chance. It was not by "chance" you lost weight. It took concentrated effort on your part and a good deal of hard work. Don't relax your efforts now! If anything, pull *in* on the reins; don't loosen them.

In order to make your maintenance program a living reality and the joy it ought to be, go back again to making out a Desire-Action Worksheet. Write your desires and the actions you are taking to fulfill these desires. Your desire is now to maintain your goal weight. What are you doing about it?

Make this apply to other areas of your life.

Here is what one woman on the Maintenance Program wrote:

DESIRE	ACTION
Stop yelling at the kids.	Begin each day praying for each of them. Choose a special scripture verse for them and repeat these throughout the day in order to be thinking God's thoughts about my children instead of my own, which may be hurtful and selfish.
	Go to bed early so I am rested.
	Be certain their duties are clearly understood and make them aware of the punishment if they do not complete these when expected. This will eliminate my hollering at them and getting myself upset.
	Pay careful attention to our diet so we are getting plenty of the B vitamins (necessary for healthy nerves). Add more calcium, too.
	Meditate on what Jesus would do if He were in my shoes. What is His thinking on this? How does He feel about my children and about our situation? He wouldn't yell. What *would* He do?

This is also a good time for you to do your *God's-Will-for-Me Chart* again. You don't want to discard these practices from your life. You should make these charts continually throughout your life in order to keep close contact with *yourself*. Remember, *you* are in control of your life. These are some tools to help you stay in control. You stay in control by keeping close contact with yourself, your feelings and your actions. Your journal is of vital importance at this point.

Reach out with your new self-control in other areas of your life. You have self-control in your eating and you'll have it in other areas, too.

Some Temptations When Going on the Maintenance Program

You won't be tempted to overeat as you once were, but you

may encounter the temptation to relax your dependence on Jesus. That is why you'll have to do something to increase your dependence upon Him. You may be tempted to say things like:

"Oh, one little piece of ___ (fattening, unhealthy food) won't hurt me. After all, I'm at my goal weight now."

"What's one helping of _____ (fattening, unhealthy food)? One helping won't hurt me."

"Maybe if I go off my program just this *once*—"

"I deserve a _____ (fattening, unhealthy food) for working so hard at losing weight."

Don't forget that it was that table loaded with cakes and cookies, that bakery window, the ice cream parlor, those desserts, gravies, rich and fattening foods that once tempted you to the point your body became ugly! Do you want to become prisoner of these foods again? *It was for freedom that Christ set you free; therefore keep standing firm and do not be subject again to a yoke of slavery.*

Make a list of the "yokes of slavery" that once held you bound. Include the reasons you overate, also. Then write how Jesus has healed the hurts that motivated you to eat.

The truth is:

One little piece of that fattening and unhealthy food may hurt you deeply. It could start you on the habits that made you fat in the first place. You're on Maintenance now. All the more reason to pull in the reins.

One helping of that fattening and unhealthy food may indeed hurt you. It's not healthy; it's fattening and your body doesn't need it. Say NO to your appetite and YES to the requirements of your body. Be good to yourself.

You're free to be thin forever, not just for a little while. Now you know how to say NO to yourself. *Make no provision for the flesh.*

The only food you deserve is the food that blesses your body and soul. The food you deserve is good, wholesome, healthy food that will make your body run the best it possibly can. You deserve the best! You are a very special child of God and you don't deserve junk for that beautiful body of yours. You worked hard at losing weight. You deserve the best!

Prayer

Father, in the name of Jesus, I am free because Jesus has set me free. I am standing firm. I will not be subject again to a yoke of slavery.

I am no longer a slave of anger, revenge, frustration, loneliness, nervousness, worry, or boredom.

I no longer eat to reward myself.

I no longer eat for comfort.

I no longer eat for "treats."

I am no longer a slave to other people's eating habits. I no longer eat unhealthy and fattening foods to please others or to avoid hurting their feelings.

I eat according to the Word of God—to glorify God in my body.

I make these statements in the name of Jesus Christ, my Lord and Savior, who redeemed me from sin and death by His own death on the cross. His blood was shed for me so that I can be free to love Him and serve Him with my whole body, soul and spirit.

I thank you, Father, in the name of Jesus, that I am free from overeating, free from gluttony, free from binging, free from fat *forever*! Free to be thin!

Thank you for my maintenance program which I begin in the name of Jesus and for your glory.

In Jesus' name, Amen.

twenty

Keeping What's Yours

Here are Mr. and Mrs. Overcomer. They are standing at the threshold of their new home, which they have spent the last several weeks and months building. It's a lifetime dream come true. They've always wanted a new house. The decorating and finishing is complete and they are ready to move in. They are so happy they want to jump for joy.

As they stand admiring the beautiful construction and finishing touches of the house, they see a storm heading their way.

They get inside the house just before the sky rips open and wind and rain assail the neighborhood. What do Mr. and Mrs. Overcomer do next? As the storm rages outside, instead of closing all windows and doors, they suddenly open them. They throw open the front door, the back doors, patio doors, and garage doors.

Then they watch as the rain ruins the wallpaper, carpeting and floors, and they cry, "Oh, poor us. Everything happens to us!" Then they drag their furniture outside and set it in the mud, crying, "Isn't this awful! Even our furniture is getting ruined in this storm."

Far-fetched? Not really. Look at yourself for a moment. You now have a new body. You're thin and gorgeous for Jesus. Your body is your beautiful new home and you've worked hard for it. When storms of temptation come your way, what are you going to do? Are you going to open the doors and windows of your heart and mind for the storms to ruin? Are you going to let temptations damage any part of your beautiful new self?

Not you!

If Mr. and Mrs. Overcomer really love their new home, they'll protect it. They'll make sure it is built well so it is able to withstand storms. They'll take care of it and be certain it is in good shape at all times. It's important because they have a big investment in it.

160

Your investment is even bigger. You've invested your life. If your home were to be destroyed, your body would not necessarily die because of it. You could go on living, although you'd have to find another home. But this isn't true with your body. If your body is destroyed, where else can you move? It's shocking how many people take better care of their homes than their precious bodies.

God has an investment in you, too.

When a strong man, fully armed, guards his own homestead, his possessions are undisturbed, but when someone stronger than he attacks him and overpowers him, he takes away from him all his armor on which he had relied, and distributes his plunder.— Luke 11:21-22

You will maintain your goal weight forever when you keep a continual guard over your mouth and your appetite. You can't assume for a minute that because you are thin you can relax and set your armor down. You're in this battle for good, you know. By now you're an experienced soldier, the kind who leads others to the victory you've achieved.

You may want to say, but when does it all end? When do I get to stop being the perpetual soldier in the battlefield of life? It's tiresome to be on guard around food forever.

Listen, it's never tiring to be in the army of God. You never get exhausted or weary when you're in the battle of the Lord with Him at the front lines right beside you. He's the winner at all times. In Him we live and move and have our being. So don't think for a moment that having your guard up against temptation will be a tiresome thing. It's not. It's invigorating! It energizes you. One OV lady who had reached her goal said, "My husband can't get over how much energy I've got. He tells me I'm a real powerhouse. How do you like that? When I was fat, I didn't have a bit of energy; I was just blah all the time."

Galatians 6:9 says, "And let us not lose heart in doing good, for in due time we shall reap if we do not grow weary." Read that verse and then tell yourself, *"Self, don't you lose heart in doing good. You've been terrific so far, now don't you lose heart. Your due time is here. Self, don't you be weary now, of all times. You made it! Your body is submitted to God! You've obeyed, you've denied yourself, you've refused fleshly indulgence. Now you have*

*a new beautiful body to glorify the Lord in. Self, you praise God
for the wisdom to stand and stay on guard!"*

Remember, that unruly old self of yours would just love to put
your wisdom to sleep right when you need it most. The cookie
platter is right in front of you and you haven't eaten lunch yet.
What harm could one little cookie do? (Bye-bye Wisdom!) What
harm could two little cookies do? (Hello Chump!) Three? Six?
After ten you lose count. Don't give me that look. It *could* happen to you. Your guard is your friend. Love yourself. Love your
wisdom and your integrity. You're a new beautiful you now.
You're no longer a chump for a plateful of cookies. Your taste is
fixed on higher things. Let the fat people eat the cookies. You eat
the Word of God and *pray* for the fat people.

Put on the full armour of God it says in Ephesians 6. Now
why does a person have to go around with the full armor of God
on anyhow? Isn't that tiring? Isn't it a bit of a bore to have to lug
around the full armor of God all the time? I mean, a person could
think of better things to do than haul around a bunch of armor
all day and night, couldn't he?

No, a person could not. Thin person, don't just put on the armor of God; put on the FULL armor of God—all of it. Cover up,
zip up, snap in, button on, hook together, tie yourself snugly, no
holes, leaks, tears or rips in the full armor of God. Satan's
schemes are to get you fat again, steal your victory, make you
miserable. He hates God and he hates you. He wants to wreck
anything that glorifies God. He'd like to break every bone in your
body—destroy you completely. He'd like to turn you into a piece
of mud and get you to curse God. He hates it that you're not fat
and ugly anymore. He hates it that you *like* yourself now.

Do you see why we are talking about the *full* armor of God?

*For our struggle is not against flesh and blood, but against the
rulers, against the powers, against the world forces of this dark-
ness, against the spiritual forces of wickedness in the heavenly
places.*—Ephesians 6:12

Your battle is not with the Twinkie or the Oreo cookie. It's
not the cheesecake that hammers on your taste buds and
screams, "EAT! EAT!" *Rulers, powers, world forces* of this dark-
ness, *spiritual forces* of wickedness in the heavenly places—these

are the ones with whom you contend! Gorgeous person, you *need* the full armor of God.

How do you do this? It's relatively simple. You stay completely honest with the Lord. You remain in complete and continual communication with Him. Stand firm, therefore, having girded your loins with truth. Gird means to encircle or bind with a belt or band. It means to surround, hem in. That's what we are to do with the truth—bind ourselves to it and in it. He is truth.

Connect yourself to heaven on a direct wire that buzzes regularly with the sound of your prayers. Talk continually to Him. Praise Him, worship Him. Keep your nose in the Word. Never leave the Word. And listen when He speaks to you.

"When I begin to stumble it's because I'm not in the Word," says an OV'er who lost 58 pounds. Again and again the same is heard from hundreds of successful OV losers.

"When I'm not in the Word, I'm liable to gain weight. I'm liable to overeat."

"It's always when I'm not faithful in reading the Word that I eat what I shouldn't.

"When I pray every day and ask the Lord to show me what to eat, when I meditate on the Scriptures and speak the living Word to myself, I don't blow it. I stand strong and girded."

So will you!

You need your Daily Power Time like you need air to breathe and water to drink. You need it like you need rest and food. You need it like you need life to live.

. . . *having put on the breastplate of righteousness.* The breastplate is your spiritual shield over your heart. Your heart is hypothetically the center of your being, the well from which spring your emotions, conscience, desires, dreams and affections. Wear righteousness like integrity.

Talk about integrity.

One successful OV'er who lost over 100 pounds went to an ice cream parlour with her husband. He was accustomed to eating gooey sundaes heaped high with ugly whipped cream. (You'll never go back to such stuff after you've experienced the joys of cottage cheese and yogurt!) He asked her to join him in his indulgence. She thought, "Well, why not? I can afford *one* scoop of ice cream[1] at 150 calories a scoop . . ." Her breastplate of righteousness was still in place, in spite of these dangerous words. She had been on her weight-loss program for over a year. She had developed new patterns, even though her old hungry nature was rearing its head in this tempting situation.

She picked up the menu and began to read—something she had long ago quit doing. She was well aware of the pitfalls of reading a menu. Menus make the worst things sound delicious. Some of them even show pictures of the foods, deadly for the overeater.

She read the descriptions of every concoction. When the waitress came to take their order, her husband ordered his gooey mess and she said, as if automatically programmed to emit heavenly utterances, "I'll have tea, please."

Beautiful words.

When you are ready spiritually to go on the maintenance portion of your weight-loss program, you are no longer *developing* beautiful eating habits, you're *living* them. This OV'er was not accustomed to eating ice cream. At one time in her life her affections were set on such things as these high-calorie desserts. Now her affections were totally possessed by Jesus. Maintaining your goal weight means to reap the benefits of the weight-loss habits you have sown.

Your feet are shod with the preparation of the gospel of peace. You're no longer stumbling around confused or bewildered. You're walking in the spirit now! You're wise, able to make fine choices! You're good to yourself. Can you praise the Lord right now as you are reading this and thank Him for your walk in the *Spirit?*

You are a partaker of His divine nature!

You have crucified the desires and passions of the flesh!

You are walking in the Spirit and your feet are wearing the truth of the Word of God!

Your shield of faith extinguishes all the flaming missiles of the evil one.

Every day when you have your Daily Power Time and you pray to the Lord about your appetite, you are exercising faith. The Lord loves your faith. *It's impossible to please Him without faith* (Heb 11:6). When you trust Him to help you with your problem of overeating, you are exercising faith that He indeed *will* help.

The cry of so many overeaters is, "How can I be a good witness for Jesus when I'm so overweight? How can I tell people that Jesus will help them with their problems when my own weight problem is so obvious?"

One woman named Sharon wrote these tragic words on a response sheet:

"One night in March of this year I was at work and talking with some of the ladies. One of the ladies was really concerned about her husband and the terrible way he treated his health. Then she started putting down everybody who smoked and drank. Well, when she left the room, the other ladies just exploded. They said, 'She's got some nerve talking about how other people harm their bodies when she's so *fat*.' I shrank in my chair because I was five feet two inches and weighed 195 pounds. These ladies knew I was a Christian and I was suddenly so ashamed of myself. I had put down people who smoked and drank, too. Here I was, no better than they were. I was killing my own body by overeating."

Then Sharon stopped feeling sorry for herself and picked up her shield of faith. She lost 26 pounds by July 31. She read about Overeaters Victorious in the newspaper, and the fellowship she found with other Christians in OV who were learning how to carry their shields of faith was the help and encouragement she needed. "I had just never learned before that God could be my strength in this area of my life," she explains.

The ladies at work didn't know how much an impact their words had on her that day back in March. They see the change in her now, though. They see that Jesus is making a difference in Sharon's life and that He is a big enough Lord to help her become thin.

Being overweight should never stop anyone from telling others about the love of Jesus! There's a popular little saying around with the initials B.P.J.I.T.W.M.Y., interpreted "Be patient, Jesus isn't through with me yet." Yes, He heals us of all our diseases, delivers us from destruction and is the Savior of mankind. He saves us from overeating!

. . . take the helmet of salvation, and the sword of the Spirit, which is the Word of God.

One OV'er who was relatively new to the program had a hairraising experience on her way to work one day. She was early and on the highway she saw on the seat beside her an almost-empty box of cookies her children had left there. She hadn't had breakfast (an OV no-no) and so she absently reached over and took one of those cookies. After she had eaten about six of them her appetite was geared up so high she could have eaten anything in sight. She decided she had enough time and she would stop at a restaurant and eat breakfast.

She'd have eggs, juice, toast, etc., etc., etc. She pulled off the highway and drove to the restaurant. She was practically breathless when she pulled into the parking lot behind the restaurant. She knew what the menu looked like with all those photos of tempting dishes. She could see the rows and rows of foods listed, she could almost smell the bacon frying in the kitchen, the pancakes sizzling on the grill. She popped out of the car and started for the door. Suddenly she heard within her the Bible verse, "Having begun with the Spirit, are you now ending with the flesh?" She stopped in her tracks. Her feet, although she didn't think so, were *still* shod with the gospel of peace. The Word of God was still her mighty sword.

"I don't have to do this thing," she told herself. "I can get back into my car and stop this binge before it starts."

Those cookies had triggered off a food-lust response in her and she could have eaten enough food for six people in one little innocent breakfast. Obviously, she wouldn't have wisely ordered a boiled egg and unbuttered wheat toast. (You don't eat wisely when you're binging.) She would have eaten like a monstrous human garbage grinder. She knew it and so did the Lord.

It was the Word that stopped her—*the Word of God*!

Soak in the Word of God so it can hold you tightly and guard you from yourself. The sword of the Spirit will slice apart and tear into shreds every sneaking lying plot to make you binge and get fat again.

She rushed back to her car and arrived at her job early. There she had her Daily Power Time with Jesus, feasting on a magnificent spiritual meal. What a wonderful victory.

Prayer

Dear Jesus, I choose to allow nothing to interfere with my relationship with you and the teaching you have brought into my life regarding eating. I completely cover myself in the armor of

God so that I am able to resist temptation and stand my ground. I tighten the belt of truth around my waist. I put on the breastplate of righteousness and integrity. I shod my feet in preparation by reading and meditating daily in God's Word. I lift up the shield of faith which comes by reading the Word of God. I quench the flaming missiles of Satan in your wonderful name.

Dear Jesus, I choose the helmet of salvation. I take the sword of the Spirit, which is the Word of God. I choose to pray at all times in the Spirit, and keep alert to those things which could destroy me.

I pray this way, dear Lord, to affirm my commitment to you and to exercise my inheritance as a child of God. In Christ I am victorious.

I love you, Jesus.

Amen.

---

1. Have you been telling yourself that ice cream is nutritious because it's a supposed milk product? Here are just a few of the more than 60 chemical additives that might be inside your favorite ice cream: carrageenan, furcelleran, agar-agar, alcin, calcium sulfate, gelatin, gum karaya, locust bean gum, oat gum, gum tragacanth, mono- and diglycerides, polysorbate 65 and 80, sodium carboxymethylcellulose, propylene glycol alginate, microcrystalline cellulose, dioctyl sodium sulfosuccinate, sodium citrate, disodium phosphate, tetrasodium pyrophosphate, sodium hexametaphosphate, calcium carbonate, magnesium carbonate, calcium oxide and hydroxide, magnesium oxide and hydroxide. These additives are used to simulate flavor, color, texture and to prevent crystal formation during storage. Ice cream does not list ingredients on the package.

If you're still singing, "I scream, you scream, we all scream for ice cream," it's time to scream a little differently. This high-calorie dessert, loaded with sugar, just isn't what you think it is.

twenty-one

How to Talk About Losing Weight Without Being an Unbearable Bore

What could be worse than being excited about something, sharing it with your friends and discovering you're boring them to pieces? What's wrong with everybody, you may wonder. Why don't they find the same fascination in discussing my lunch as I do?—two boiled egg whites, three radishes, four sliced carrots, two celery sticks and three tablespoons of cottage cheese. Where is the drum roll when I talk about how I always cut off all the skin and fat from my broiled chicken and never, no NEVER, eat my veggies with butter or margarine?

Why doesn't everybody else hear the same heavenly choir I do when I announce I'm one and three-fourths pounds lighter than I was this very minute last Tuesday? Has the world become so calloused they can't even appreciate my lovely breakfasts of skim milk, one tablespoon of wheat germ, a half grapefruit and vitamin supplements?

Not only is a person who talks endlessly about his diet a bore to other people, he or she is usually a self-styled trumpeter for the stomachs of the world. You wouldn't dare eat a baked potato in front of some dieters (even though you've wisely omitted the butter and dolloped a tablespoon of cottage cheese on top) because they would evil-eye you until you lost your appetite. An evil eye is that insidious blank expression on a person's face that says, "Good grief, are you really going to eat *that?*"

You're an Overeater Victorious. You've got it together. People need only look at you to see that: you're free from the bondage of fattening and unhealthy food, you're gorgeous all over. Why, it's *obvious.*

You don't need to evil-eye anyone's greasy hamburger or get on a soap box to preach against the sins of gluttony at the next holiday celebration you attend.

People will not only be observing a thinner you, they will clearly observe a happier you. This is because when a person lives in obedience to God, he becomes a happier person. There's no happier place to be than in obedience to the will of God.

You knew from the beginning that your overeating was a spiritual problem. This is humbling. You don't ever want this divine liberating knowledge to turn sour in your heart by pointing an accusing finger at other fat people. Bless them and have compassion. Have compassion on yourself, too. Have mercy. Jesus does.

The only way to share the love and goodness of the Lord is to do it in love. Jesus doesn't throw poisoned darts at obese people. He says, "Come unto *Me,* all ye who are heavy laden. . . ." He doesn't condemn and turn His back on those who eat the wrong foods. He says simply, "*I* am the bread of life!"

Eating healthy foods shouldn't become doctrine. Primary doctrine must always be Christ crucified, risen and coming again. He came to set us free, and we must take care not to tie ourselves into knots over the evils of unhealthy food in the world. "Be *wise* as serpents, *harmless* as doves," He tells us.

OV members are instructed not to campaign for OV and not to seek to recruit new members. "Talk about Jesus," they are told, "not OV. Lead your friends to Jesus. That's our purpose." If people are brought to an Overeaters Victorious meeting against their will, they become rebellious and angry because they resent anyone telling them they should stop eating so much.

Love is something you *do.* You *do* act kindly. You *do* encourage others. You *do* give your time and energy to help someone else. You *do* act as though other people's bodies are as important as yours.

One OV woman had been attacking alcoholics for years until she realized 1 Corinthians 3:16 and 17 pertained to her as well as the alcoholics of the world. "Do you not know that you are a temple of God and that the Spirit of God dwells in you?" These words inspired her to lose 60 extra pounds of fat.

Losing weight and changing your eating habits for the glory of God gives you a merciful and an understanding heart toward others. It never makes you judgmental, accusing or haughty.

For the whole law concerning human relationships is complied with in this one precept, YOU SHALL LOVE YOUR NEIGHBOR AS YOURSELF.—Galatians 5:14

This is who you are. This is the kind of person you are.

You are called to freedom.

You do not let your freedom be an incentive to your flesh.

You are the kind of person who loves yourself and others.

You serve others through the resources you have gained by spending time alone with God.

You seek ways to be loving and helpful to those around you.

You are a person of strength and compassion.

You do nothing of yourself but through the Lord.

You act in love purely under the direction of the Holy Spirit.

You care about other people and don't find fault with other fat people.

You don't find fault with people who are still eating junk food and hurting their bodies. You have mercy and compassion, and you earnestly pray for help and guidance for them.

You are an Overeater Victorious—free to be thin!

The words of the Overeater Victorious are no longer, "I am a failure"; they are, "I AM VICTORIOUS!"

I Am Victorious

Today I walk in victory. I am totally victorious over food. I do not abuse food or use it for satisfaction, reward or emotional outlet. I do not express my anger or frustration by overeating.

Jesus alone satisfies me. Jesus alone gives me strength to handle anger, frustration, and to live up to my daily responsibilities. I need no other reward than to walk in a covenant of obedience with Him. He is God, my Father. He is my Savior in the person of Jesus Christ. He is my helper in the person of the Holy Spirit.

I worship God today in obedience, praise and positive attitudes. I am loved by God. I also love and respect myself. Jesus died for me and has forgiven all my sins. I am entitled to the best of life because Jesus died to give it to me.

I have put off the works of the flesh and clothed myself in the righteousness of Christ. The Holy Spirit empowers me to be free *not* to eat the foods that make me fat. I will be thin in the name of Jesus and for His glory.

He is mine and I am His completely. I use the Word of God as my weapon for battle. I fight winning battles and do not surrender to junk foods and the works of the flesh. I choose to walk in the Spirit by the power of God which He infuses into me.

I AM VICTORIOUS!

twenty-two

Food for Thought

Usually an overweight person wants to be much thinner than he really ought to be. A woman who now weighs 275 pounds dreams of weighing a mere 105 pounds one day. The thought of it is so impossible and exhausting to her she runs to the refrigerator for something to eat to "calm her nerves." Perhaps the Lord would have her ideal weight at 145, which is still a long way off, but not quite so far off as 105 pounds.

To maintain your weight at 105 pounds a day, you would eat no more than 1,680 calories a day. If your ideal weight is 145 pounds, you would eat no more than 2,320 calories a day in order to maintain that weight.

Here's how it works. Figure out your ideal weight (after consultation with the Lord) and multiply that by 16.

Example: Your ideal weight is 135. Multiply it by 16 and you get 2,160. That's how many calories you can consume a day to maintain your ideal weight.

Your ideal weight times 16 is the number of calories you may eat to *maintain* your ideal weight.

You're not losing any weight yet, though. In order to lose one pound of stored fat, you have to omit 4,000 calories somewhere in your diet. If your "maintaining" calorie allowance is 2,160 calories a day and you eat only 1,000 calories a day, you have cut out 8,120 calories a week. When you do that, you will have lost over two pounds! In a month's time you will drop almost ten pounds.

Many dieters don't have a solid understanding of these facts. It's easy to remember them, though, if you (1) multiply your ideal weight by 16 for the calories you'll eat a day to *maintain* that weight, (2) subtract the number of calories you are now eating each day to lose weight, and (3) figure how much you'll be losing by the 4,000 calories equals one pound formula.

More "Free To Be Thin" Helps!

Soft drinks. Try replacing your soft drinks, coffee and tea with delicious healthy fruit juices. Discover the beauties of plain water! You'd be amazed at how happy children can be with a glass of water when they're thirsty.

Tea and coffees. Some people think tea is healthier to drink than coffee. Actually, commercial tea contains caffeine, too, just as coffee does. It also has tannic acid in it, harmful to your health. Another deception is that decaffeinated coffee is better for you than regular coffee. The National Cancer Institute announced the chemical, *trichloroethylene or TCE,* used in making decaffeinated coffee, causes cancer in the liver of mice. It served a warning of a possible cancer danger to humans.

Instant tea contains malto dextrin, citric acid, artificial color and flavor, vegetable oil and BHA (a preservative). Ouch!

Hot chocolate and cocoa. Chocolate and cocoa contain caffeine from the cocoa bean. "Dutch" cocoa doesn't mean it comes from Holland; it means it's treated with alkali. Prepared cocoa mixes are loaded with unwanted additives. *Cara-Coa* is a good substitute. It's made of carob and contains no caffeine.

Herb teas. Drink herb teas in moderation. There are dozens to choose from and you'll love them. Carry a packet of herb tea-bags in your pocket or purse for quick hot drinks when you are away from home. Just ask the waiter or your host for a cup of hot water and *voila!* An instant and refreshing drink. You no longer have to put coffee, commercial teas or soda pop into your precious body.

The food scaries. You are not bound to a list of *never eat these.* You're free to eat the foods you know to be good for your body. As Christians we must not allow fear to have any part of our lives. This includes the area of food. We choose to *bless* our bodies at all times. Fear never motivates us, love does. We aren't afraid of the food we eat; we're in *control* of it.

Eating healthy is easier on the budget. You *can* afford healthy food! A bag of apples costs no more than a half gallon of ice cream. Frozen sugarless fruit juices cost no more than the six-packs of sugary soda pop you've been buying. Fresh fruit and natural foods are actually less expensive when you consider the price of potato chips, commercial chip dips, packaged cakes, jello and other junk foods. You'll be saving on your food bills when you eat healthy natural foods. It's a fact.

Snacks. If you've had enough for the day, don't even nibble on the carrots and celery in the refrigerator. Your body doesn't need carrots and celery if it's had its fill, so there's no reason to nibble on any food, even if it is low-cal. That may sound cruel, but your body will thank you for it. You're in control!

Oils. Do keep oil in your diet. Use safflower oil. Use it in your salad dressings. Mix one tablespoon with lemon juice or apple cider vinegar and whatever seasonings you like. Safflower oil is a good source of lecithin, vitamin E and linoleic acid, all necessary to keep you young and energetic. The oil will help prevent water retention in your tissues and will also aid in losing weight by causing your body to change sugar to fat at a slower rate. The oil in your diet lessens your cravings for sweets and prevents hunger pangs because it causes food to remain in your stomach longer. Do not omit oil from your diet, but do not substitute animal fat, grease or other oils for safflower oil.

Eating out. Remember, don't read the menu when you go to a restaurant. *Plan ahead* what you'll order before you get there. If you're not sure the restaurant serves food you can eat, call first. Ask if they serve salads, vegetables without butter, unbreaded seafood broiled without butter, lean meats, fresh fruits; most restaurants are glad to be helpful. If you're going to a banquet, a luncheon, a dinner or something similar where the food is already prepared and you'll be expected to eat what is served you, pray before going, "Lord, let there be something there I can eat." There will usually be something you can eat without piling on the calories. If nothing else, your tossed salad ought to be safe. Don't even look at the dessert. Give it to a neighbor at the table immediately or have the waiter remove it. Don't eat your meal staring at a dessert. You don't hate yourself anymore.

Artificials and chemicals. Avoid foods with artificial sweeteners, chemicals, dough conditioners, preservatives, artificial *any*thing. We'll get you healthy yet.

Sugar and your children. The younger your children are, the easier it can be to eliminate sugar from their diet. William Dufty, the author of *Sugar Blues,* says that if children are raised completely without sugar, when they are exposed to the multiple temptations of a sugared culture, they will have developed natural immunity. Given sugar, candy or sweetened soft drinks, they reject them. Don't feed the baby sugared baby foods and sugared drinks. Low blood sugar, or eating too much sugar, produces the following symptoms in children as well as in adults: overeating, loss of memory, nightmares, bedwetting, sleepwalking, hyperactivity, nervousness, irritability, lethargy and mental fatigue. It has long been known that sugar causes hyperactivity in children. Omit sugar from the diet of your child and your child will be healthier, happier, have fewer colds and infections and have better abilities in his schoolwork.

The human body has no nutritional need for refined table sugar. It has been linked to almost every major disease from diabetes and heart ailments to cancer. Sugar is added to canned soups, sauces, canned vegetables, baked beans, catsup, table salt, pickles, processed meats, rice mixtures, peanut butter, crackers—virtually *all* convenience and fast foods.

When you read labels, be aware that these words mean harmful sugar: Dextrose, sucrose, fructose, maltose, lactose and even the word carbohydrate. If you want to be sure the product you buy has no sugar, look for the words, "No sugar added."

Raw sugar, brown sugar. Sorry, these are no better than refined white sugar. Raw sugar is simply the dirty sugar before it's further refined. Use raw honey and pure maple syrup instead.

Share foods. Some foods are share foods. There are too many calories in them for one person alone. An avocado is such a food. It is meant to be shared because one person shouldn't eat all those 275 calories alone. Baked goods prepared with all natural ingredients, including unrefined whole wheat flour and honey, safflower oil, nuts, dried unsulphured fruits and eggs, are meant to be shared. Food so delicious and nutritious should be shared.

Leftovers. Never eat the leftovers after a meal. You need them less than the garbage disposal does. Sometimes it's wise to throw them away rather than store them in the refrigerator. It may sound wasteful in this day of ecology, but those little dabs of this and that in your refrigerator will somehow find their way to your stomach if you don't get rid of them.

Kiddie food. Get rid of the kiddie food you've been addicted to. Ever notice how fat people still eat the food little children are attracted to? Twinkies, cupcakes, ice cream, pizza, soda pop, macaroni and cheese, hot dogs, fudge, candy, mashed potatoes, french fries, hamburgers—ugh! If you are an adult person, your tastes should have changed somewhat by now. A slightly different version of 1 Corinthians 13:11 could read, "When I was a child I ate as a child. But now I am an adult. I choose to eat wisely with nutrition and health in mind." *Now that I'm a grown up person I put away childish foods!* Bless your heart (liver, lungs, bones, brain and blood, too) as you chuck the old fattening junk for the new beautiful healthy array of food for your body which God gave to you, healthy natural foods.

Measure foods. Don't panic. You won't have to carry around a scale and a set of measuring cups in your back pocket. You need to get acquainted with what a half cup of something looks like, though. It's important that you know how much a cup is or how a quarter of a cup of something looks. That's why you have to measure. If 1-1/2 ounces of parmesan cheese has 170 calories, you'll need to know what it *looks* like before you can count it. One woman was shocked when she saw what a half cup of peas looked like on her plate. *You must measure your food for at least three weeks.* In three weeks' time you should know what certain measurements look like. Keep your scale and cups handy to check with periodically after that. Good-bye fat, hello gorgeous!

Steaming food. A delicious way to serve vegetables is to steam them. Buy a steamer to set in your pan, add approximately an inch of water to bottom of pan and you'll have delicious, crisp and tasty vegetables. You don't even need to add butter.

Enjoy your food. Don't take the fun out of eating. Eating is no sin. Gluttony is sin. Lust is sin. Disobedience is sin. Enjoying what God gives you blesses Him. That's one of the reasons why we thank Him for our daily bread. He gives it to us to bless our bodies. It's proper to enjoy what He gives us. For the overweight person, enjoyment of food has been like a god. *That* is sin. For you, Free To Be Thin! person, eating is no longer sin—it's stewardship of your body. It's the means God is using to show you obedience, love and discipline so that you will have a fulfilled and beautiful life in Christ.

Here is a simplified guideline for you to use in your food plan.

Be sure to eat from every food category or group to insure you're getting proper vitamins, minerals and protein for each day. You are the one responsible to the Lord for what you are eating and how much each day. You adjust the portions of each food group to fit into your daily calorie allotment. You do not cut out one type of good nutritious food group to allow yourself more in another food group. You are a responsible self-controlled person. You eat in balance.

Blessings!

Overeaters Victorious Recommended Diet Guideline—The Simple Way to Eat

Breakfast:
    High Vitamin C fruit
    Protein food—choose one
        2 oz. cottage or pot cheese
        1 oz. hard cheese
        2 oz. cooked or canned fish
        1 egg
        8-oz. cup skimmed milk
    Whole grain bread or cereal
    Beverage

Lunch:
    Protein food—choose one
        2 oz fish, poultry or lean meat
        4 oz. cottage or pot cheese
        2 oz. hard cheese
        1 egg
        2 level tablespoons peanut butter
    Whole grain bread
    Vegetables—raw or cooked
    Fruit—1 serving
    Beverage

Dinner:
    Protein food—choose one:
        4 oz. cooked fish, poultry or lean meat

Vegetables—cooked or raw
   High Vitamin A
   Potato
   Other vegetables—you may eat freely.
Fruit—1 serving
Beverage

Other daily foods:
   Fat—choose 3 daily
   Milk—2 cups (8 oz. each) skimmed

Remember: measure quantities of each serving and count every calorie.

Prayer

Lord Jesus, help me to use these helps to the glory of God. I choose to be a faithful steward of my body. I shall faithfully measure and count the calories I put into my body. I shall become the person you have intended me to be since the beginning of time. I choose a walk of obedience, mercy, love and discipline. Thank you, Lord, for being my enabler, my strength, my motivator, my true love, my friend, my comforter, my King of kings and my Lord.

I love you. From your "Free To Be Thin!" person,

_____

(your name)

Tomorrow

"Can you help my friend?" asked the voice on the other end of the wire. "If she doesn't lose weight, she's going to die."

"What do you mean, she's going to die?"

The answer was strained but emphatic. "She weighs 525 pounds!"

Her name is Helen and she is 400 pounds overweight. Her doctor has told her that her heart is going to give out if she keeps gaining. Already, her breathing is labored and difficult and her heartbeat irregular.

Her obesity has caused her the loss of the use of her legs. She is confined to a custom-made wheelchair and rarely leaves her apartment. The only clothes she owns are a couple of enormous tent dresses large enough to drape across her body, and some thongs for her feet. Her rolls and rolls of fat rubbing against itself has given her body running sores which do not heal. Her skin, releasing toxins and poisons, causes her apartment to reek with putrid, foul smells.

Where is hope? she wants to know. She had been considering a bi-pass operation where her intestines would be sealed off so that the food she eats will pass right through the bowels twenty minutes after she's eaten. But she's afraid of the surgery and doesn't want it.

Everything she has tried, including pills, shots, diets, even hypnosis and fasting, has not worked. She can't get out of her apartment to attend the many diet clubs and weight loss groups available because moving is so laborious. It's difficult to get into a car and she is too fat to walk. Her doctor and friends know she'll die if she doesn't lose weight.

With 400 pounds to lose, Helen needs a miracle!

She doesn't want to have the bi-pass surgery and is desperate enough to try anything but that. She will even give Jesus a try.

An OV chapter leader visited Helen with her Bible and OV materials. The 525-pound woman said, "I know Jesus is my last and only hope." She gave her heart to Him and prayed with her new friend (who had lost 70 pounds and was still losing).

Immediately prayer requests were made across the country to other OV losers for Helen. Her fellow losers have her name up on their refrigerator doors, bathroom mirrors, office walls, in their wallets and other places to remind them of her and to pray for her throughout the day. She is not alone in her battle against her extra 400 pounds. Others are standing with her.

Helen began to lose weight and in three weeks' time lost 30 pounds. She knows it will be a long term process. She's planning a three-year program, but she is willing to work at it. In Christ, she has found her miracle.

It is to the Helens of this world and every one of us who has ever struggled with fat that Jesus reaches His loving arms out in help and love.

We will all of us hear Him say one day:

Behold, you are beautiful, my love,
Behold, you are beautiful! . . .
I will hie me to the mountain of myrrh
and the hill of frankincense.
You are all fair, my love;
there is no flaw in you.

—Song of Solomon 4:1, 6, 7, RSV

Prayer

Lord Jesus, I know you love me in whatever shape I'm in, but I thank you with my whole heart that I am free to have self-control and a thin body now.

I choose to be beautiful, fair and without flaw as you tell me I am. I choose to be disciplined and thin in the name of Jesus. Thank you, Jesus, for setting me free to be thin. Amen.

A closing note from Neva Coyle:

That feeling you are feeling now is *hope*. Please don't suppress it. It's beautiful. It's *yours*. When I was over a hundred pounds overweight, I felt that same feeling. It was frightening, but at the same time, wonderful. Would I ever *really* be thin? Was it really possible for someone like me who had never been thin in her life?

Now my goal has been reached and my dream to be thin has come true. If you will follow the precepts set forth for you in this book, your dream will come true for you, too. You *will* be thin and once you are, you will be *thin forever!*

I'm praying for you!

Neva Coyle

Bibliography

Brown, Raysa Rose. *How to Be a Thin Person*. New York: Random House, 1977.

Dufty, William. *Sugar Blues*. New York: Warner Books, 1975.

Goldbeck, Nikki and David. *The Dieter's Companion*. New York: Signet New American Library, 1975.

Goldbeck, Nikki and David. *The Supermarket Handbook*. New York: Signet New American Library, 1973.

Jeffrey, D. Balfour and Katz, Roger C. *Take It Off and Keep It Off*. New Jersey: Prentice-Hall, Inc., 1977.

Kerr, Graham. *The New Seasoning*. New York: Simon and Schuster, 1976.

Kordel, Lelord. *Eat and Grow Slender*. New York: Manor Books, 1962.

Null, Gary and Steve. *Protein for Vegetarians*. New York: Jove HBJ Books, 1974.

Stuart, Richard B. and Davis, Barbara. *Slim Chance in a Fat World—Behavioral Control of Obesity*. Illinois: Research Press, 1972.

Waters, Ethel. *To Me It's Wonderful*. New York: Harper and Row, 1972.

Watson, Dr. George. *Nutrition and Your Mind*. New York: Harper and Row, 1972.

Books by Marie Chapian

POETRY:

City Psalms (Moody Press, 1972)
Mind Things (Creation House, 1973)

GIFT BOOKS:

To My Friend Books, series of 12 Christian gift books (Successful Living, 1974)

CHILDREN'S BOOKS:

Mustard Seed Library (Creation House, 1974)
The Holy Spirit and Me
I Learn About the Fruit of the Holy Spirit
I Learn About the Gifts of the Holy Spirit

BIOGRAPHY:

The Emancipation of Robert Sadler (Bethany Fellowship, Inc., 1975)
Of Whom the World Was Not Worthy (Bethany Fellowship, Inc., 1978)
In the Morning of My Life, the story of singer, Tom Netherton (Tyndale House, 1979)

PSYCHOLOGY:

Telling Yourself the Truth, with William Backus, a self-help handbook on Christian psychology (Bethany Fellowship, Inc., 1980)

Books by Neva Coyle:

Free To Be Thin, w/Marie Chapian, a successful weight-loss plan which links learning how to eat with how to live

There's More To Being Thin Than Being Thin, w/Marie Chapian, focusing on the valuable lessons learned on the *journey* to being thin

Slimming Down and Growing Up, w/Marie Chapian, applying the "Free To Be Thin" principles to kids

Living Free, her personal testimony

Daily Thoughts on Living Free, a devotional

Scriptures for Living Free, a counter-top display book of Scriptures to accompany the devotional

Free To Be Thin Cookbook, a collection of tasty, nutritious recipes complete with the calorie content of each

Free To Be Thin Leader's Kit, a step-by-step guide for organizing and leading an Overeaters Victorious group, including five cassette tapes of instruction

Free To Be Thin Daily Planner, a three-month planner for recording daily thoughts, activities and calorie intake

Tape Albums and Study Guides by Neva Coyle:

(The study guides come with the tape albums but may also be ordered separately.)

A Seminar on Living Free (four cassettes) A recording of her seminar in which she shares the principles that have helped her break free from a life of misery and self-satisfaction
Living Free Study Guide, to accompany the tape album

Free To Be Thin (four cassettes) Victory, Weight-loss, Deliverance
Free To Be Thin Study Guide No. 1, Getting Started, to be used with the book by the same title, and/or the tape album

Discipline (four cassettes) A Program for Spiritual Fitness
Free To Be Thin Study Guide No. 2, Discipline, to be used with the book by the same title, and/or the tape album

Abiding (four cassettes) Honesty in Relationships
Abiding Study Guide

Freedom (four cassettes) Escape from the Ordinary
Freedom Study Guide

Diligence (four cassettes) Overcoming Discouragement
Diligence Study Guide

Obedience (four cassettes) Developing a Listening Heart
Obedience Study Guide

Free To Be Thin Aerobics, available in LP record album with booklet, or cassette tape album with booklet

Restoration (three cassettes) Helping restore those who may have faltered in their spiritual life or commitment
Restoration Study Guide

Perseverance (four cassettes) For People Under Pressure
Perseverance Study Guide